THE CRIMES
OF ENGLAND

By

G. K. CHESTERTON

First published in 1915

Read &' Co.

Copyright © 2020 Read & Co. History

This edition is published by Read & Co. History,
an imprint of Read & Co.

This book is copyright and may not be reproduced or copied in any
way without the express permission of the publisher in writing.

British Library Cataloguing-in-Publication Data
A catalogue record for this book is available
from the British Library.

Read & Co. is part of Read Books Ltd.
For more information visit
www.readandcobooks.co.uk

CONTENTS

G. K. Chesterton

Gilbert Keith Chesterton was an English journalist and author, who came of a family of estate-agents. He was born in London on the 29th of May 1874. He was educated at St Paul's school, which he left in 1891 with the idea of studying art. But his natural bent was literary, and he devoted himself mainly to cultivating that means of expression, both in prose and verse; he did occasional reviewing, and had some experience in a publisher's office. In 1900, having already produced a volume of clever poems, *The Wild Knight*, he definitely took to journalism as a career, and became a regular contributor of signed articles to the Liberal journals, the *Speaker* and *Daily News*. He established himself from the first as a writer with a distinct personality, combative to a swashbuckling degree, unconventional and dogmatic; and the republication of much of his work in a series of volumes (*e.g. Twelve Types, Heretics, Orthodoxy*), characterized by much acuteness of criticism, a pungent style, and the capacity of laying down the law with unflagging impetuosity and humour, enhanced his reputation.

His powers as a writer are best shown in his studies of Browning (in the "English Men of Letters" series) and of Dickens; but these were only rather more ambitious essays among a medley of characteristic utterances, ranging from fiction (including *The Napoleon of Notting-hill*) to fugitive verse, and from artistic criticism to discussions of ethics and religion.

The interest excited by his work and views was indicated and analysed in an anonymous volume (*G. K. Chesterton: a Criticism*) published in 1908.

A biography from
1911, *Encyclopædia Britannica, Volume 6*

THE CRIMES OF ENGLAND

CHAPTER I

SOME WORDS TO PROFESSOR WHIRLWIND

DEAR PROFESSOR WHIRLWIND,

Your name in the original German is too much for me; and this is the nearest I propose to get to it: but under the majestic image of pure wind marching in a movement wholly circular I seem to see, as in a vision, something of your mind. But the grand isolation of your thoughts leads you to express them in such words as are gratifying to yourself, and have an inconspicuous or even an unfortunate effect upon others. If anything were really to be made of your moral campaign against the English nation, it was clearly necessary that somebody, if it were only an Englishman, should show you how to leave off professing philosophy and begin to practise it. I have therefore sold myself into the Prussian service, and in return for a cast-off suit of the Emperor's clothes (the uniform of an English midshipman), a German hausfrau's recipe for poison gas, two penny cigars, and twenty-five Iron Crosses, I have consented to instruct you in the rudiments of international controversy. Of this part of my task I have here little to say that is not covered by a general adjuration to you to observe certain elementary rules. They are, roughly speaking, as follows:—

First, stick to one excuse. Thus if a tradesman, with whom your social relations are slight, should chance to find you toying with the coppers in his till, you may possibly explain that you are interested in Numismatics and are a Collector of Coins; and he may possibly believe you. But if you tell him afterwards that you pitied him for being overloaded with unwieldy copper discs, and were in the act of replacing them by a silver sixpence of your own, this further explanation, so far from increasing his confidence in your motives, will (strangely enough) actually decrease it. And if you are so unwise as to be struck by yet another brilliant idea, and tell him that the pennies were all bad pennies, which you were concealing to save him from a police prosecution for coining, the tradesman may even be so wayward as to institute a police prosecution himself. Now this is not in any way an exaggeration of the way in which you have knocked the bottom out of any case you may ever conceivably have had in such matters as the sinking of the *Lusitania*. With my own eyes I have seen the following explanations, apparently proceeding from your pen, (i) that the ship was a troop-ship carrying soldiers from Canada; (ii) that if it wasn't, it was a merchant-ship unlawfully carrying munitions for the soldiers in France; (iii) that, as the passengers on the ship had been warned in an advertisement, Germany was justified in blowing them to the moon; (iv) that there were guns, and the ship had to be torpedoed because the English captain was just going to fire them off; (v) that the English or American authorities, by throwing the *Lusitania* at the heads of the German commanders, subjected them to an insupportable temptation; which was apparently somehow demonstrated or intensified by the fact that the ship came up to schedule time, there being some mysterious principle by which having tea at tea-time justifies poisoning the tea; (vi) that the ship was not sunk by the Germans at all but by the English, the English captain having deliberately tried to drown himself and some thousand of his own countrymen in order to cause an exchange of stiff notes between Mr. Wilson and the

Kaiser. If this interesting story be true, I can only say that such frantic and suicidal devotion to the most remote interests of his country almost earns the captain pardon for the crime. But do you not see, my dear Professor, that the very richness and variety of your inventive genius throws a doubt upon each explanation when considered in itself? We who read you in England reach a condition of mind in which it no longer very much matters what explanation you offer, or whether you offer any at all. We are prepared to hear that you sank the *Lusitania* because the sea-born sons of England would live more happily as deep-sea fishes, or that every person on board was coming home to be hanged. You have explained yourself so completely, in this clear way, to the Italians that they have declared war on you, and if you go on explaining yourself so clearly to the Americans they may quite possibly do the same.

Second, when telling such lies as may seem necessary to your international standing, do not tell the lies to the people who know the truth. Do not tell the Eskimos that snow is bright green; nor tell the negroes in Africa that the sun never shines in that Dark Continent. Rather tell the Eskimos that the sun never shines in Africa; and then, turning to the tropical Africans, see if they will believe that snow is green. Similarly, the course indicated for you is to slander the Russians to the English and the English to the Russians; and there are hundreds of good old reliable slanders which can still be used against both of them. There are probably still Russians who believe that every English gentleman puts a rope round his wife's neck and sells her in Smithfield. There are certainly still Englishmen who believe that every Russian gentleman takes a rope to his wife's back and whips her every day. But these stories, picturesque and useful as they are, have a limit to their use like everything else; and the limit consists in the fact that they are not *true*, and that there necessarily exists a group of persons who know they are not true. It is so with matters of fact about which you asseverate so positively to us, as if they were matters of opinion. Scarborough might be a fortress; but it is not. I happen to know it is not. Mr. Morel may deserve to be universally admired in England; but he is not universally admired in England. Tell the Russians that he is by all means; but do not tell us. We have seen him; we have also seen Scarborough. You should think of this before you speak.

Third, don't perpetually boast that you are cultured in language which proves that you are not. You claim to thrust yourself upon everybody on the ground that you are stuffed with wit and wisdom, and have enough for the whole world. But people who have wit enough for the whole world, have wit enough for a whole newspaper paragraph. And you can seldom get through even a whole paragraph without being monotonous, or irrelevant, or unintelligible, or self-contradictory, or broken-minded generally. If you have something to teach us, teach it to us now. If you propose to convert us after you have conquered us, why not convert us before you have conquered us? As it is, we cannot believe what you say about your superior education because of the way in which you say it. If an Englishman says, "I don't make no mistakes in English, not me," we can understand his remark; but we cannot endorse it. To say, "Je parler le Frenche language, non demi," is comprehensible, but not convincing. And when you say, as you did in a recent appeal to the Americans, that the Germanic Powers have sacrificed a great deal of "red fluid" in defence of their culture, we point out to you that cultured people do not employ such a literary style. Or when you say that the Belgians were so ignorant as to think they were being butchered when they weren't, we only wonder whether *you* are so ignorant as to think you are being believed when you aren't. Thus, for instance, when you brag about burning Venice to express your contempt for "tourists," we cannot think much of the culture, as culture, which supposes St. Mark's to be a thing for tourists instead of historians. This, however, would be the least part of our unfavourable judgment. That judgment is complete when we have read such a paragraph as this, prominently displayed in a paper in which you specially spread yourself: "That the Italians have a perfect knowledge of the fact that this city of antiquities and tourists is subject, and rightly subject, to attack and bombardment, is proved by the measures they took at the beginning of the war to remove some of their greatest art treasures." Now culture may or may not include the power to admire antiquities, and to restrain oneself from the pleasure of breaking them like toys. But culture does, presumably, include the power to think. For less laborious intellects than your own it is generally sufficient to think once. But if you will think twice or twenty times, it cannot but dawn on you that there is something wrong in the reasoning by which the placing of diamonds in a safe proves that they are "rightly subject" to a burglar. The incessant assertion of such things can do little to spread your superior culture; and if you say them too often people may even begin to doubt whether you have any superior culture after all. The earnest friend now advising you cannot but grieve at such incautious garrulity. If you confined yourself to single words, uttered at intervals of about a month or so, no one could possibly raise any rational objection, or subject them to any rational criticism. In time you might come to use whole sentences without revealing the real state of things.

Through neglect of these maxims, my dear Professor, every one of your attacks upon England has gone wide. In pure fact they have not touched the spot, which the real critics of England know to be a very vulnerable spot. We have a real critic of England in Mr. Bernard Shaw, whose name you parade but apparently cannot spell; for in the paper to which I have referred he is called Mr. Bernhard Shaw. Perhaps you think he and Bernhardi are the same man. But if you quoted Mr. Bernard Shaw's statement instead of misquoting his name, you would find that his criticism of England is exactly the opposite of your own; and naturally, for it is a rational criticism. He does not blame England for being against Germany. He does most definitely blame England for not being sufficiently firmly and emphatically on the side of Russia. He is not such a fool as to accuse Sir Edward Grey of being a fiendish Machiavelli plotting against Germany; he accuses him of being an amiable aristocratic stick who failed to frighten the Junkers from their plan of war. Now, it is not in the least a question of whether we happen to like this quality or that: Mr. Shaw, I rather fancy, would dislike such verbose compromise more than downright plotting. It is simply the fact that Englishmen like Grey are open to Mr. Shaw's attack and are not open to yours. It is not true that the English were sufficiently clearheaded or self-controlled to conspire for the destruction of Germany. Any man who knows England, any man who hates England as one hates a living thing, will tell you it is not true. The English may be snobs, they may be plutocrats, they may be hypocrites, but they are not, as a fact, plotters; and I gravely doubt whether they could be if they wanted to. The mass of the people are perfectly incapable of plotting at all, and if the small ring of rich people who finance our politics were plotting for anything, it was for peace at almost any price. Any Londoner who knows the London streets and newspapers as he knows the Nelson column or the Inner Circle, knows that there were men in the governing class and in the Cabinet who were literally thirsting to defend Germany until Germany, by her own act, became indefensible. If they said nothing in support of the tearing up of the promise of peace to Belgium, it is simply because there was nothing to be said.

You were the first people to talk about World-Politics; and the first people to disregard them altogether. Even your foreign policy is domestic policy. It does not even apply to any people who are not Germans; and of your wild guesses about some twenty other peoples, not one has gone right even by accident. Your two or three shots at my own not immaculate land have been such that you would have been much nearer the truth if you had tried to invade England by crossing the Caucasus, or to discover England among the South Sea Islands. With your first delusion, that our courage was calculated and malignant when in truth our very corruption was timid and confused, I have already dealt. The case is the same with your second favourite phrase; that the British army is mercenary. You learnt it in books and not in battlefields; and I should like to be present at a scene in which you tried to bribe the most miserable little loafer in Hammersmith as if he were a cynical condottiere selling his spear to some foreign city. It is not the fact, my dear sir. You have been misinformed. The British Army is not at this moment a hireling army any more than it is a conscript army. It is a volunteer army in the strict sense of the word; nor do I object to your calling it an amateur army. There is no compulsion, and there is next to no pay. It is at this moment drawn from every class of the community, and there are very few classes which would not earn a little more money in their ordinary trades. It numbers very nearly as many men as it would if it were a conscript army; that is with the necessary margin of men unable to serve or needed to serve otherwise. Ours is a country in which that democratic spirit which is common to Christendom is rather unusually sluggish and far below the surface. And the most genuine and purely popular movement that we have had since the Chartists has been the enlistment for this war. By all means say that such vague and sentimental volunteering is valueless in war if you think so; or even if you don't think so. By all means say that Germany is unconquerable and that we cannot really kill you. But if you say that we do not really want to kill you, you do us an injustice. You do indeed.

I need not consider the yet crazier things that some of you have said; as that the English intend to keep Calais and fight France as well as Germany for the privilege of purchasing a frontier and the need to keep a conscript army. That, also, is out of books, and pretty mouldy old books at that. It was said, I suppose, to gain sympathy among the French, and is therefore not my immediate business, as they are eminently capable of looking after themselves. I merely drop one word in passing, lest you waste your powerful intellect on such projects. The English may some day forgive you; the French never will. You Teutons are too light and fickle to understand the Latin seriousness. My only concern is to point out that about England, at least, you are invariably and miraculously wrong.

Now speaking seriously, my dear Professor, it will not do. It could be easy to fence with you for ever and parry every point you attempt to make, until English people began to think there was nothing wrong with England at all. But I refuse to play for safety in this way. There is a very great deal that is really wrong with England, and it ought not to be forgotten even in the full blaze of your marvellous mistakes. I cannot have my countrymen tempted to those pleasures of intellectual pride which are the result of comparing themselves with you. The deep collapse and yawning chasm of your ineptitude leaves me upon a perilous spiritual elevation. Your mistakes are matters of fact; but to enumerate them does not exhaust the truth. For instance, the learned man who rendered the phrase in an English advertisement "cut you dead" as "hack you to death," was in error; but to say that many such advertisements are vulgar is not an error. Again, it is true that the English poor are harried and insecure, with insufficient instinct for armed revolt, though you will be wrong if you say that they are occupied literally in shooting the moon. It is true that the average Englishman is too much attracted by aristocratic society; though you will be in error if you quote dining with Duke Humphrey as an example of it. In more ways than one you forget what is meant by idiom.

I have therefore thought it advisable to provide you with a catalogue of the real crimes of England; and I have selected them on a principle which cannot fail to interest and please you. On many occasions we have been very wrong indeed. We were very wrong indeed when we took part in preventing Europe from putting a term to the impious piracies of Frederick the Great. We were very wrong indeed when we allowed the triumph over Napoleon to be soiled with the mire and blood of Blucher's sullen savages. We were very wrong indeed when we allowed the peaceful King of Denmark to be robbed in broad daylight by a brigand named Bismarck; and when we allowed the Prussian swashbucklers to enslave and silence the French provinces which they could neither govern nor persuade. We were very wrong indeed when we flung to such hungry adventurers a position so important as Heligoland. We were very wrong indeed when we praised the soulless Prussian education and copied the soulless Prussian laws. Knowing that you will mingle your tears with mine over this record of English wrong-doing, I dedicate it to you, and I remain,

Yours reverently,

G. K. CHESTERTON

CHAPTER II

THE PROTESTANT HERO

A question is current in our looser English journalism touching what should be done with the German Emperor after a victory of the Allies. Our more feminine advisers incline to the view that he should be shot. This is to make a mistake about the very nature of hereditary monarchy. Assuredly the Emperor William at his worst would be entitled to say to his amiable Crown Prince what Charles II. said when his brother warned him of the plots of assassins: "They will never kill me to make you king." Others, of greater monstrosity of mind, have suggested that he should be sent to St. Helena. So far as an estimate of his historical importance goes, he might as well be sent to Mount Calvary. What we have to deal with is an elderly, nervous, not unintelligent person who happens to be a Hohenzollern; and who, to do him justice, does think more of the Hohenzollerns as a sacred caste than of his own particular place in it. In such families the old boast and motto of hereditary kingship has a horrible and degenerate truth. The king never dies; he only decays for ever.

If it were a matter of the smallest importance what happened to the Emperor William when once his house had been disarmed, I should satisfy my fancy with another picture of his declining years; a conclusion that would be peaceful, humane, harmonious, and forgiving.

In various parts of the lanes and villages of South England the pedestrian will come upon an old and quiet public-house, decorated with a dark and faded portrait in a cocked hat and the singular inscription, "The King of Prussia." These inn signs probably commemorate the visit of the Allies after 1815, though a great part of the English middle classes may well have connected them with the time when Frederick II. was earning his title of the Great, along with a number of other territorial titles to which he had considerably less claim. Sincere and simple-hearted Dissenting ministers would dismount before that sign (for in those days Dissenters drank beer like Christians, and indeed manufactured most of it) and would pledge the old valour and the old victory of him whom they called the Protestant Hero. We should be using every word with literal exactitude if we said that he was really something devilish like a hero. Whether he was a Protestant hero or not can be decided best by those who have read the correspondence of a writer calling himself Voltaire, who was quite shocked at Frederick's utter lack of religion of any kind. But the little Dissenter drank his beer in all innocence and rode on. And the great blasphemer of Potsdam would have laughed had he known; it was a jest after his own heart. Such was the jest he made when he called upon the emperors to come to communion, and partake of the eucharistic body of Poland. Had he been such a Bible reader as the Dissenter doubtless thought him, he might haply have foreseen the vengeance of humanity upon his house. He might have known what Poland was and was yet to be; he might have known that he ate and drank to his damnation, discerning not the body of God.

Whether the placing of the present German Emperor in charge of one of these wayside public-houses would be a jest after *his* own heart possibly remains to be seen. But it would be much more melodious and fitting an end than any of the sublime euthanasias which his enemies provide for him. That old sign creaking above him as he sat on the bench outside his home of exile would be a much more genuine memory of the real greatness of his race than the modern and almost gimcrack stars and garters that were pulled in Windsor Chapel. From modern knighthood has departed all shadow of chivalry; how far we have travelled from it can easily be tested by the mere suggestion that Sir Thomas Lipton, let us say, should wear his lady's sleeve round his hat or should watch his armour in the Chapel of St. Thomas of Canterbury. The giving and receiving of the Garter among despots and diplomatists is now only part of that sort of pottering mutual politeness which keeps the peace in an insecure and insincere state of society. But that old blackened wooden sign is at least and after all the sign of something; the sign of the time when one solitary Hohenzollern did not only set fire to fields and cities, but did truly set on fire the minds of men, even though it were fire from hell.

Everything was young once, even Frederick the Great. It was an appropriate preface to the terrible epic of Prussia that it began with an unnatural tragedy of the loss of youth. That blind and narrow savage who was the boy's father had just sufficient difficulty in stamping out every trace of decency in him, to show that some such traces must have been there. If the younger and greater Frederick ever had a heart, it was a broken heart; broken by the same blow that broke his flute. When his only friend was executed before his eyes, there were two corpses to be borne away; and one to be borne on a high war-horse through victory after victory: but with a small bottle of poison in the pocket. It is not irrelevant thus to pause upon the high and dark house of his childhood. For the peculiar quality which marks out Prussian arms and ambitions from all others of the kind consists in this wrinkled and premature antiquity. There is something comparatively boyish about the triumphs of all the other tyrants. There was something better than ambition in the beauty and ardour of the young Napoleon. He was at least a lover; and his first campaign was like a love-story. All that was pagan in him worshipped the Republic as men worship a woman, and all that was Catholic in him understood the paradox of Our Lady of Victories. Henry VIII., a far less reputable person, was in his early days a good knight of the later and more florid school of chivalry; we might almost say that he was a fine old English gentleman so long as he was young. Even Nero was loved in his first days: and there must have been some cause to make that Christian maiden cast flowers on his dishonourable grave. But the spirit of the great Hohenzollern smelt from the first of the charnel. He came out to his first victory like one broken by defeats; his strength was stripped to the bone and fearful as a fleshless resurrection; for the worst of what could come had already befallen him. The very construction of his kingship was built upon the destruction of his manhood. He had known the final shame; his soul had surrendered to force. He could not redress that wrong; he could only repeat it and repay it. He could make the souls of his soldiers surrender to his gibbet and his whipping-post; he could 'make the souls of the nations surrender to his soldiers. He could only break men in as he had been broken; while he could break in, he could never break out. He could not slay in anger, nor even sin with simplicity. Thus he stands alone among the conquerors of their kind; his madness was not due to a mere misdirection of courage. Before the whisper of war had come to him the foundations of his audacity had been laid in fear.

Of the work he did in this world there need be no considerable debate. It was romantic, if it be romantic that the dragon should swallow St. George. He turned a small country into a great one: he made a new diplomacy by the fulness and far-flung daring of his lies: he took away from criminality all reproach of carelessness and incompleteness. He achieved an amiable combination of thrift and theft. He undoubtedly gave to stark plunder something of the solidity of property. He protected whatever he stole as simpler men protect whatever they have earned or inherited. He turned his hollow eyes with a sort of loathsome affection upon the territories which had most reluctantly become his: at the end of the Seven Years' War men knew as little how he was to be turned out of Silesia as they knew why he had ever been allowed in it. In Poland, like a devil in possession, he tore asunder the body he inhabited; but it was long before any man dreamed that such disjected limbs could live again. Nor were the effects of his break from Christian tradition confined to Christendom; Macaulay's world-wide generalisation is very true though very Macaulayese. But though, in a long view, he scattered the seeds of war all over the world, his own last days were passed in a long and comparatively prosperous peace; a peace which received and perhaps deserved a certain praise: a peace with which many European peoples were content. For though he did not understand justice, he could understand moderation. He was the most genuine and the most wicked of pacifists. He did not want any more wars. He had tortured and beggared all his neighbours; but he bore them no malice for it.

The immediate cause of that spirited disaster, the intervention of England on behalf of the new Hohenzollern throne, was due, of course, to the national policy of the first William Pitt. He was the kind of man whose vanity and simplicity are too easily overwhelmed by the obvious. He saw nothing in a European crisis except a war with France; and nothing in a war with France except a repetition of the rather fruitless glories of Agincourt and Malplaquet. He was of the Erastian Whigs, sceptical but still healthy-minded, and neither good enough nor bad enough to understand that even the war of that irreligious age was ultimately a religious war. He had not a shade of irony in his whole being; and beside Frederick, already as old as sin, he was like a rather brilliant schoolboy.

But the direct causes were not the only causes, nor the true ones. The true causes were connected with the triumph of one of the two traditions which had long been struggling in England. And it is pathetic to record that the foreign tradition was then represented by two of the ablest men of that age, Frederick of Prussia and Pitt; while what was really the old English tradition was represented by two of the stupidest men that mankind ever tolerated in any age, George III. and Lord Bute. Bute was

the figurehead of a group of Tories who set about fulfilling the
fine if fanciful scheme for a democratic monarchy sketched by
Bolingbroke in "The Patriot King." It was bent in all sincerity on
bringing men's minds back to what are called domestic affairs,
affairs as domestic as George III. It might have arrested the
advancing corruption of Parliaments and enclosure of country-
sides, by turning men's minds from the foreign glories of the
great Whigs like Churchill and Chatham; and one of its first
acts was to terminate the alliance with Prussia. Unfortunately,
whatever was picturesque in the piracy of Potsdam was beyond
the imagination of Windsor. But whatever was prosaic in
Potsdam was already established at Windsor; the economy of
cold mutton, the heavy-handed taste in the arts, and the strange
northern blend of boorishness with etiquette. If Bolingbroke's
ideas had been applied by a spirited person, by a Stuart, for
example, or even by Queen Elizabeth (who had real spirit along
with her extraordinary vulgarity), the national soul might have
broken free from its new northern chains. But it was the irony of
the situation that the King to whom Tories appealed as a refuge
from Germanism was himself a German.

We have thus to refer the origins of the German influence in
England back to the beginning of the Hanoverian Succession;
and thence back to the quarrel between the King and the
lawyers which had issue at Naseby; and thence again to the
angry exit of Henry VIII. from the mediaeval council of Europe.
It is easy to exaggerate the part played in the matter by that great
and human, though very pagan person, Martin Luther. Henry
VIII. was sincere in his hatred for the heresies of the German
monk, for in speculative opinions Henry was wholly Catholic;
and the two wrote against each other innumerable pages, largely
consisting of terms of abuse, which were pretty well deserved
on both sides. But Luther was not a Lutheran. He was a sign
of the break-up of Catholicism; but he was not a builder of
Protestantism. The countries which became corporately and
democratically Protestant, Scotland, for instance, and Holland,

followed Calvin and not Luther. And Calvin was a Frenchman; an unpleasant Frenchman, it is true, but one full of that French capacity for creating official entities which can really act, and have a kind of impersonal personality, such as the French Monarchy or the Terror. Luther was an anarchist, and therefore a dreamer. He made that which is, perhaps, in the long run, the fullest and most shining manifestation of failure; he made a name. Calvin made an active, governing, persecuting thing, called the Kirk. There is something expressive of him in the fact that he called even his work of abstract theology "The Institutes."

In England, however, there were elements of chaos more akin to Luther than to Calvin. And we may thus explain many things which appear rather puzzling in our history, notably the victory of Cromwell not only over the English Royalists but over the Scotch Covenanters. It was the victory of that more happy-go-lucky sort of Protestantism, which had in it much of aristocracy but much also of liberty, over that logical ambition of the Kirk which would have made Protestantism, if possible, as constructive as Catholicism had been. It might be called the victory of Individualist Puritanism over Socialist Puritanism. It was what Milton meant when he said that the new presbyter was an exaggeration of the old priest; it was his *office* that acted, and acted very harshly. The enemies of the Presbyterians were not without a meaning when they called themselves Independents. To this day no one can understand Scotland who does not realise that it retains much of its mediæval sympathy with France, the French equality, the French pronunciation of Latin, and, strange as it may sound, is in nothing so French as in its Presbyterianism.

In this loose and negative sense only it may be said that the great modern mistakes of England can be traced to Luther. It is true only in this, that both in Germany and England a Protestantism softer and less abstract than Calvinism was found useful to the compromises of courtiers and aristocrats; for every abstract creed does something for human equality. Lutheranism in Germany rapidly became what it is to-day—a religion of court chaplains. The reformed church in England became something better; it became a profession for the younger sons of squires. But these parallel tendencies, in all their strength and weakness, reached, as it were, symbolic culmination when the mediæval monarchy was extinguished, and the English squires gave to what was little more than a German squire the damaged and diminished crown.

It must be remembered that the Germanics were at that time used as a sort of breeding-ground for princes. There is a strange process in history by which things that decay turn into the very opposite of themselves. Thus in England Puritanism began as the hardest of creeds, but has ended as the softest; soft-hearted and not unfrequently soft-headed. Of old the Puritan in war was certainly the Puritan at his best; it was the Puritan in peace whom no Christian could be expected to stand. Yet those Englishmen to-day who claim descent from the great militarists of 1649 express the utmost horror of militarism. An inversion of an opposite kind has taken place in Germany. Out of the country that was once valued as providing a perpetual supply of kings small enough to be stop-gaps, has come the modern menace of the one great king who would swallow the kingdoms of the earth. But the old German kingdoms preserved, and were encouraged to preserve, the good things that go with small interests and strict boundaries, music, etiquette, a dreamy philosophy, and so on. They were small enough to be universal. Their outlook could afford to be in some degree broad and many-sided. They had the impartiality of impotence. All this has been utterly reversed, and we find ourselves at war with a Germany whose powers are the widest and whose outlook is the narrowest in the world.

It is true, of course, that the English squires put themselves over the new German prince rather than under him. They put the crown on him as an extinguisher. It was part of the plan that the new-comer, though royal, should be almost rustic. Hanover must be one of England's possessions and not England one of Hanover's. But the fact that the court became a German court prepared the soil, so to speak; English politics were already subconsciously committed to two centuries of the belittlement of France and the gross exaggeration of Germany. The period can be symbolically marked out by Carteret, proud of talking German at the beginning of the period, and Lord Haldane, proud of talking German at the end of it. Culture is already almost beginning to be spelt with a k. But all such pacific and only slowly growing Teutonism was brought to a crisis and a decision when the voice of Pitt called us, like a trumpet, to the rescue of the Protestant Hero.

Among all the monarchs of that faithless age, the nearest to a man was a woman. Maria Theresa of Austria was a German of the more generous sort, limited in a domestic rather than a national sense, firm in the ancient faith at which all her own courtiers were sneering, and as brave as a young lioness. Frederick hated her as he hated everything German and everything good. He sets forth in his own memoirs, with that clearness which adds something almost superhuman to the mysterious vileness of his character, how he calculated on her youth, her inexperience and her lack of friends as proof that she could be despoiled with safety. He invaded Silesia in advance of his own declaration of war (as if he had run on ahead to say it was coming) and this new anarchic trick, combined with the corruptibility of nearly all the other courts, left him after the two Silesian wars in possession of the stolen goods. But Maria Theresa had refused to submit to the immorality of nine points of the law. By appeals and concessions to France, Russia, and other powers, she contrived to create something which, against the atheist innovator even in that atheist age, stood up for an instant like a spectre of the Crusades. Had that Crusade been universal and whole-hearted, the great new precedent of mere force and fraud would have been broken; and the whole appalling judgment which is fallen upon Christendom would have passed us by. But the other Crusaders were only half in earnest for Europe; Frederick was quite in earnest for Prussia; and he sought for allies, by whose aid this weak revival of good might be stamped out, and his adamantine impudence endure for ever. The allies he found were the English. It is not pleasant for an Englishman to have to write the words.

This was the first act of the tragedy, and with it we may leave Frederick, for we are done with the fellow though not with his work. It is enough to add that if we call all his after actions satanic, it is not a term of abuse, but of theology. He was a Tempter. He dragged the other kings to "partake of the body of Poland," and learn the meaning of the Black Mass. Poland lay prostrate before three giants in armour, and her name passed into a synonym for failure. The Prussians, with their fine magnanimity, gave lectures on the hereditary maladies of the man they had murdered. They could not conceive of life in those limbs; and the time was far off when they should be undeceived. In that day five nations were to partake not of the body, but of the spirit of Poland; and the trumpet of the resurrection of the peoples should be blown from Warsaw to the western isles.

CHAPTER III

THE ENIGMA OF WATERLOO

That great Englishman Charles Fox, who was as national as Nelson, went to his death with the firm conviction that England had made Napoleon. He did not mean, of course, that any other Italian gunner would have done just as well; but he did mean that by forcing the French back on their guns, as it were, we had made their chief gunner necessarily their chief citizen. Had the French Republic been left alone, it would probably have followed the example of most other ideal experiments; and praised peace along with progress and equality. It would almost certainly have eyed with the coldest suspicion any adventurer who appeared likely to substitute his personality for the pure impersonality of the Sovereign People; and would have considered it the very flower of republican chastity to provide a Brutus for such a Caesar. But if it was undesirable that equality should be threatened by a citizen, it was intolerable that it should be simply forbidden by a foreigner. If France could not put up with French soldiers she would very soon have to put up with Austrian soldiers; and it would be absurd if, having decided to rely on soldiering, she had hampered the best French soldier even on the ground that he was not French. So that whether we regard Napoleon as a hero rushing to the country's help, or a tyrant profiting by the country's extremity, it is equally clear that those who made the war made the war-lord; and those who tried to destroy the Republic were those who created the Empire. So, at least, Fox argued against that much less English prig who would have called him unpatriotic; and he threw the blame upon

Pitt's Government for having joined the anti-French alliance, and so tipped up the scale in favour of a military France. But whether he was right or no, he would have been the readiest to admit that England was not the first to fly at the throat of the young Republic. Something in Europe much vaster and vaguer had from the first stirred against it. What was it then that first made war—and made Napoleon? There is only one possible answer: the Germans. This is the second act of our drama of the degradation of England to the level of Germany. And it has this very important development; that Germany means by this time *all* the Germans, just as it does to-day. The savagery of Prussia and the stupidity of Austria are now combined. Mercilessness and muddleheadedness are met together; unrighteousness and unreasonableness have kissed each other; and the tempter and the tempted are agreed. The great and good Maria Theresa was already old. She had a son who was a philosopher of the school of Frederick; also a daughter who was more fortunate, for she was guillotined. It was natural, no doubt, that her brother and relatives should disapprove of the incident; but it occurred long after the whole Germanic power had been hurled against the new Republic. Louis XVI. himself was still alive and nominally ruling when the first pressure came from Prussia and Austria, demanding that the trend of the French emancipation should be reversed. It is impossible to deny, therefore, that what the united Germanics were resolved to destroy was the reform and not even the Revolution. The part which Joseph of Austria played in the matter is symbolic. For he was what is called an enlightened despot, which is the worst kind of despot. He was as irreligious as Frederick the Great, but not so disgusting or amusing. The old and kindly Austrian family, of which Maria Theresa was the affectionate mother, and Marie Antoinette the rather uneducated daughter, was already superseded and summed up by a rather dried-up young man self-schooled to a Prussian efficiency. The needle is already veering northward. Prussia is already beginning to be the captain of the Germanics "in shining armour." Austria is already becoming a loyal *sekundant*.

But there still remains one great difference between Austria and Prussia which developed more and more as the energy of the young Napoleon was driven like a wedge between them. The difference can be most shortly stated by saying that Austria did, in some blundering and barbaric way, care for Europe; but Prussia cared for nothing but Prussia. Austria is not a nation; you cannot really find Austria on the map. But Austria is a kind of Empire; a Holy Roman Empire that never came, an expanding and contracting-dream. It does feel itself, in a vague patriarchal way, the leader, not of a nation, but of nations. It is like some dying Emperor of Rome in the decline; who should admit that the legions had been withdrawn from Britain or from Parthia, but would feel it as fundamentally natural that they should have been there, as in Sicily or Southern Gaul. I would not assert that the aged Francis Joseph imagines that he is Emperor of Scotland or of Denmark; but I should guess that he retains some notion that if he did rule both the Scots and the Danes, it would not be more incongruous than his ruling both the Hungarians and the Poles. This cosmopolitanism of Austria has in it a kind of shadow of responsibility for Christendom. And it was this that made the difference between its proceedings and those of the purely selfish adventurer from the north, the wild dog of Pomerania.

It may be believed, as Fox himself came at last to believe, that Napoleon in his latest years was really an enemy to freedom, in the sense that he was an enemy to that very special and occidental form of freedom which we call Nationalism. The resistance of the Spaniards, for instance, was certainly a popular resistance. It had that peculiar, belated, almost secretive strength with which war is made by the people. It was quite easy for a conqueror to get into Spain; his great difficulty was to get out again. It was one of the paradoxes of history that he who had turned the mob into an army, in defence of its rights against the princes, should at last have his army worn down, not by princes but by mobs. It is equally certain that at the other end of Europe, in burning

Moscow and on the bridge of the Beresina, he had found the common soul, even as he had found the common sky, his enemy. But all this does not affect the first great lines of the quarrel, which had begun before horsemen in Germanic uniform had waited vainly upon the road to Varennes or had failed upon the miry slope up to the windmill of Valmy. And that duel, on which depended all that our Europe has since become, had great Russia and gallant Spain and our own glorious island only as subordinates or seconds. That duel, first, last, and for ever, was a duel between the Frenchman and the German; that is, between the citizen and the barbarian.

It is not necessary nowadays to defend the French Revolution, it is not necessary to defend even Napoleon, its child and champion, from criticisms in the style of Southey and Alison, which even at the time had more of the atmosphere of Bath and Cheltenham than of Turcoing and Talavera. The French Revolution was attacked because it was democratic and defended because it was democratic; and Napoleon was not feared as the last of the iron despots, but as the first of the iron democrats. What France set out to prove France has proved; not that common men are all angels, or all diplomatists, or all gentlemen (for these inane aristocratic illusions were no part of the Jacobin theory), but that common men can all be citizens and can all be soldiers; that common men can fight and can rule. There is no need to confuse the question with any of those escapades of a floundering modernism which have made nonsense of this civic common-sense. Some Free Traders have seemed to leave a man no country to fight for; some Free Lovers seem to leave a man no household to rule. But these things have not established themselves either in France or anywhere else. What has been established is not Free Trade or Free Love, but Freedom; and it is nowhere so patriotic or so domestic as in the country from which it came. The poor men of France have not loved the land less because they have shared it. Even the patricians are patriots; and if some honest Royalists or aristocrats are still saying that

29

democracy cannot organise and cannot obey, they are none the less organised by it and obeying it, nobly living or splendidly dead for it, along the line from Switzerland to the sea.

But for Austria, and even more for Russia, there was this to be said; that the French Republican ideal was incomplete, and that they possessed, in a corrupt but still positive and often popular sense, what was needed to complete it. The Czar was not democratic, but he was humanitarian. He was a Christian Pacifist; there is something of the Tolstoyan in every Russian. It is not wholly fanciful to talk of the White Czar: for Russia even destruction has a deathly softness as of snow. Her ideas are often innocent and even childish; like the idea of Peace. The phrase Holy Alliance was a beautiful truth for the Czar, though only a blasphemous jest for his rascally allies, Metternich and Castlereagh. Austria, though she had lately fallen to a somewhat treasonable toying with heathens and heretics of Turkey and Prussia, still retained something of the old Catholic comfort for the soul. Priests still bore witness to that mighty mediaeval institution which even its enemies concede to be a noble nightmare. All their hoary political iniquities had not deprived them of that dignity. If they darkened the sun in heaven, they clothed it with the strong colours of sunrise in garment or gloriole; if they had given men stones for bread, the stones were carved with kindly faces and fascinating tales. If justice counted on their shameful gibbets hundreds of the innocent dead, they could still say that for them death was more hopeful than life for the heathen. If the new daylight discovered their vile tortures, there had lingered in the darkness some dim memory that they were tortures of Purgatory and not, like those which Parisian and Prussian diabolists showed shameless in the sunshine, of naked hell. They claimed a truth not yet disentangled from human nature; for indeed earth is not even earth without heaven, as a landscape is not a landscape without the sky. And in, a universe without God there is not room enough for a man.

It may be held, therefore, that there must in any case have come a conflict between the old world and the new; if only because the old are often broad, while the young are always narrow. The Church had learnt, not at the end but at the beginning of her centuries, that the funeral of God is always a premature burial. If the bugles of Bonaparte raised the living populace of the passing hour, she could blow that yet more revolutionary trumpet that shall raise all the democracy of the dead. But if we concede that collision was inevitable between the new Republic on the one hand and Holy Russia and the Holy Roman Empire on the other, there remain two great European forces which, in different attitudes and from very different motives, determined the ultimate combination. Neither of them had any tincture of Catholic mysticism. Neither of them had any tincture of Jacobin idealism. Neither of them, therefore, had any real moral reason for being in the war at all. The first was England, and the second was Prussia.

It is very arguable that England must, in any case, have fought to keep her influence on the ports of the North Sea. It is quite equally arguable that if she had been as heartily on the side of the French Revolution as she was at last against it, she could have claimed the same concessions from the other side. It is certain that England had no necessary communion with the arms and tortures of the Continental tyrannies, and that she stood at the parting of the ways. England was indeed an aristocracy, but a liberal one; and the ideas growing in the middle classes were those which had already made America, and were remaking France. The fiercest Jacobins, such as Danton, were deep in the liberal literature of England. The people had no religion to fight for, as in Russia or La Vendée. The parson was no longer a priest, and had long been a small squire. Already that one great blank in our land had made snobbishness the only religion of South England; and turned rich men into a mythology. The effect can be well summed up in that decorous abbreviation by which our rustics speak of "Lady's Bedstraw," where they once spoke of "Our Lady's Bedstraw." We have dropped the comparatively democratic adjective, and kept the aristocratic noun. South England is still, as it was called in the Middle Ages, a garden; but it is the kind where grow the plants called "lords and ladies."

We became more and more insular even about our continental conquests; we stood upon our island as if on an anchored ship. We never thought of Nelson at Naples, but only eternally at Trafalgar; and even that Spanish name we managed to pronounce wrong. But even if we regard the first attack upon Napoleon as a national necessity, the general trend remains true. It only changes the tale from a tragedy of choice to a tragedy of chance. And the tragedy was that, for a second time, we were at one with the Germans.

But if England had nothing to fight for but a compromise, Prussia had nothing to fight for but a negation. She was and is, in the supreme sense, the spirit that denies. It is as certain that she was fighting against liberty in Napoleon as it is that she was fighting against religion in Maria Theresa. What she was fighting for she would have found it quite impossible to tell you. At the best, it was for Prussia; if it was anything else, it was tyranny. She cringed to Napoleon when he beat her, and only joined in the chase when braver people had beaten him. She professed to restore the Bourbons, and tried to rob them while she was restoring them. For her own hand she would have wrecked the Restoration with the Revolution. Alone in all that agony of peoples, she had not the star of one solitary ideal to light the night of her nihilism.

The French Revolution has a quality which all men feel; and which may be called a sudden antiquity. Its classicalism was not altogether a cant. When it had happened it seemed to have happened thousands of years ago. It spoke in parables; in the hammering of spears and the awful cap of Phrygia. To some it seemed to pass like a vision; and yet it seemed eternal as a group of statuary. One almost thought of its most strenuous figures as naked. It is always with a shock of comicality that we remember that its date was so recent that umbrellas were fashionable and top-hats beginning to be tried. And it is a curious fact, giving a kind of completeness to this sense of the thing as something that happened outside the world, that its first great act of arms and also its last were both primarily symbols; and but for this visionary character, were in a manner vain. It began with the taking of the old and almost empty prison called the Bastille; and we always think of it as the beginning of the Revolution, though the real Revolution did not come till some time after. And it ended when Wellington and Blucher met in 1815; and we always think of it as the end of Napoleon; though Napoleon had really fallen before. And the popular imagery is right, as it generally is in such things: for the mob is an artist, though not a man of science. The riot of the 14th of July did not specially deliver prisoners inside the Bastille, but it did deliver the prisoners outside. Napoleon when he returned was indeed a *revenant*, that is, a ghost. But Waterloo was all the more final in that it was a spectral resurrection and a second death. And in this second case there were other elements that were yet more strangely symbolic. That doubtful and double battle before Waterloo was like the dual personality in a dream. It corresponded curiously to the double mind of the Englishman. We connect Quatre Bras with things romantically English to the verge of sentimentalism, with Byron and "The Black Brunswicker." We naturally sympathise with Wellington against Ney. We do not sympathise, and even then we did not really sympathise, with Blucher against Napoleon. Germany has complained that we passed over lightly the presence of Prussians at the decisive action. And well we might. Even at the time our sentiment was not solely jealousy, but very largely shame. Wellington, the grimmest and even the most unamiable of Tories, with no French sympathies and not enough human ones, has recorded his opinion of his Prussian allies in terms of curt disgust. Peel, the primmest and most snobbish Tory that ever praised "our gallant Allies" in a frigid official speech, could not contain himself about the conduct of Blucher's men. Our middle classes did well to adorn their parlours with the picture of the "Meeting of Wellington and Blucher." They should have hung up a companion piece of Pilate and Herod shaking hands. Then, after that meeting amid the ashes of Hougomont, where they dreamed they had trodden out the embers of all democracy, the Prussians rode on before, doing after their kind. After them went that ironical aristocrat out of embittered Ireland, with what thoughts we know; and Blucher, with what thoughts we care not; and his soldiers entered Paris, and stole the sword of Joan of Arc.

CHAPTER IV

THE COMING OF THE JANISSARIES

The late Lord Salisbury, a sad and humorous man, made many public and serious remarks that have been proved false and perilous, and many private and frivolous remarks which were valuable and ought to be immortal. He struck dead the stiff and false psychology of "social reform," with its suggestion that the number of public-houses made people drunk, by saying that there were a number of bedrooms at Hatfield, but they never made him sleepy. Because of this it is possible to forgive him for having talked about "living and dying nations": though it is of such sayings that living nations die. In the same spirit he included the nation of Ireland in the "Celtic fringe" upon the west of England. It seems sufficient to remark that the fringe is considerably broader than the garment. But the fearful satire of time has very sufficiently avenged the Irish nation upon him, largely by the instrumentality of another fragment of the British robe which he cast away almost contemptuously in the North Sea. The name of it is Heligoland; and he gave it to the Germans.

The subsequent history of the two islands on either side of England has been sufficiently ironical. If Lord Salisbury had foreseen exactly what would happen to Heligoland, as well as to Ireland, he might well have found no sleep at Hatfield in one bedroom or a hundred. In the eastern isle he was strengthening a fortress that would one day be called upon to destroy us. In the western isle he was weakening a fortress that would one day be called upon to save us. In that day his trusted ally, William Hohenzollern, was to batter our ships and boats from the Bight of Heligoland; and in that day his old and once-imprisoned enemy, John Redmond, was to rise in the hour of English jeopardy, and be thanked in thunder for the free offer of the Irish sword. All that Robert Cecil thought valueless has been our loss, and all that he thought feeble our stay. Among those of his political class or creed who accepted and welcomed the Irish leader's alliance, there were some who knew the real past relations between England and Ireland, and some who first felt them in that hour. All knew that England could no longer be a mere mistress; many knew that she was now in some sense a suppliant. Some knew that she deserved to be a suppliant. These were they who knew a little of the thing called history; and if they thought at all of such dead catchwords as the "Celtic fringe" for a description of Ireland, it was to doubt whether we were worthy to kiss the hem of her garment. If there be still any Englishman who thinks such language extravagant, this chapter is written to enlighten him.

In the last two chapters I have sketched in outline the way in which England, partly by historical accident, but partly also by false philosophy, was drawn into the orbit of Germany, the centre of whose circle was already at Berlin. I need not recapitulate the causes at all fully here. Luther was hardly a heresiarch for England, though a hobby for Henry VIII. But the negative Germanism of the Reformation, its drag towards the north, its quarantine against Latin culture, was in a sense the beginning of the business. It is well represented in two facts; the barbaric refusal of the new astronomical calendar merely because it was invented by a Pope, and the singular decision to pronounce Latin as if it were something else, making it not a dead language but a new language. Later, the part played by particular royalties is complex and accidental; "the furious German" came and passed; the much less interesting Germans came and stayed. Their influence was negative but not negligible; they kept England out of that current of European life into which the Gallophil Stuarts might have carried her. Only one of the

Hanoverians was actively German; so German that he actually gloried in the name of Briton, and spelt it wrong. Incidentally, he lost America. It is notable that all those eminent among the real Britons, who spelt it right, respected and would parley with the American Revolution, however jingo or legitimist they were; the romantic conservative Burke, the earth-devouring Imperialist Chatham, even, in reality, the jog-trot Tory North. The intractability was in the Elector of Hanover more than in the King of England; in the narrow and petty German prince who was bored by Shakespeare and approximately inspired by Handel. What really clinched the unlucky companionship of England and Germany was the first and second alliance with Prussia; the first in which we prevented the hardening tradition of Frederick the Great being broken up by the Seven Years' War; the second in which we prevented it being broken up by the French Revolution and Napoleon. In the first we helped Prussia to escape like a young brigand; in the second we helped the brigand to adjudicate as a respectable magistrate. Having aided his lawlessness, we defended his legitimacy. We helped to give the Bourbon prince his crown, though our allies the Prussians (in their cheery way) tried to pick a few jewels out of it before he got it. Through the whole of that period, so important in history, it must be said that we were to be reckoned on for the support of unreformed laws and the rule of unwilling subjects. There is, as it were, an ugly echo even to the name of Nelson in the name of Naples. But whatever is to be said of the cause, the work which we did in it, with steel and gold, was so able and strenuous that an Englishman can still be proud of it. We never performed a greater task than that in which we, in a sense, saved Germany, save that in which a hundred years later, we have now, in a sense, to destroy her. History tends to be a facade of faded picturesqueness for most of those who have not specially studied it: a more or less monochrome background for the drama of their own day. To these it may well seem that it matters little whether we were on one side or the other in a fight in which all the figures are antiquated; Bonaparte and Blucher are both in old cocked hats; French kings and French regicides are both not only dead men but dead foreigners; the whole is a tapestry as decorative and as arbitrary as the Wars of the Roses. It was not so: we fought for something real when we fought for the old world against the new. If we want to know painfully and precisely what it was, we must open an old and sealed and very awful door, on a scene which was called Ireland, but which then might well have been called hell.

Having chosen our part and made war upon the new world, we were soon made to understand what such spiritual infanticide involved; and were committed to a kind of Massacre of the Innocents. In Ireland the young world was represented by young men, who shared the democratic dream of the Continent, and were resolved to foil the plot of Pitt; who was working a huge machine of corruption to its utmost to absorb Ireland into the Anti-Jacobin scheme of England. There was present every coincidence that could make the British rulers feel they were mere abbots of misrule. The stiff and self-conscious figure of Pitt has remained standing incongruously purse in hand; while his manlier rivals were stretching out their hands for the sword, the only possible resort of men who cannot be bought and refuse to be sold. A rebellion broke out and was repressed; and the government that repressed it was ten times more lawless than the rebellion. Fate for once seemed to pick out a situation in plain black and white like an allegory; a tragedy of appalling platitudes. The heroes were really heroes; and the villains were nothing but villains. The common tangle of life, in which good men do evil by mistake and bad men do good by accident, seemed suspended for us as for a judgment. We had to do things that not only were vile, but felt vile. We had to destroy men who not only were noble, but looked noble. They were men like Wolfe Tone, a statesman in the grand style who was not suffered to found a state; and Robert Emmet, lover of his land and of a woman, in whose very appearance men saw something of the eagle grace of the young Napoleon. But he was luckier than the young Napoleon; for he has remained young. He was hanged; not before he had uttered one of those phrases that are the hinges of history. He made an epitaph of the refusal of an epitaph: and with a gesture has hung his tomb in heaven like Mahomet's coffin. Against such Irishmen we could only produce Castlereagh; one of the few men in human records who seem to have been made famous solely that they might be infamous. He sold his own country, he oppressed ours; for the rest he mixed his metaphors, and has saddled two separate and sensible nations with the horrible mixed metaphor called the Union. Here there is no possible see-saw of sympathies as there can be between Brutus and Caesar or between Cromwell and Charles I.: there is simply nobody who supposes that Emmet was out for worldly gain, or that Castlereagh was out for anything else. Even the incidental resemblances between the two sides only served to sharpen the contrast and the complete superiority of the nationalists. Thus, Castlereagh and Lord Edward Fitzgerald were both aristocrats. But Castlereagh was the corrupt gentleman at the Court, Fitzgerald the generous gentleman upon the land; some portion of whose blood, along with some portion of his spirit, descended to that great gentleman, who—in the midst of the emetic immoralism of our modern politics—gave back that land to the Irish peasantry. Thus again, all such eighteenth-century aristocrats (like aristocrats almost anywhere) stood apart from the popular mysticism and the shrines of the poor; they were theoretically Protestants, but practically pagans. But Tone was the type of pagan who refuses to persecute, like Gallio: Pitt was the type of pagan who consents to persecute; and his place is with Pilate. He was an intolerant indifferentist; ready to enfranchise the Papists, but more ready to massacre them. Thus, once more, the two pagans, Tone and Castlereagh, found a pagan end in suicide. But the circumstances were such that any man, of any party, felt that Tone had died like Cato and Castlereagh had died like Judas.

The march of Pitt's policy went on; and the chasm between light and darkness deepened. Order was restored; and wherever order spread, there spread an anarchy more awful than the sun has ever looked on. Torture came out of the crypts of the Inquisition and walked in the sunlight of the streets and fields. A village vicar was slain with inconceivable stripes, and his corpse set on fire with frightful jests about a roasted priest. Rape became a mode of government. The violation of virgins became a standing order of police. Stamped still with the same terrible symbolism, the work of the English Government and the English settlers seemed to resolve itself into animal atrocities against the wives and daughters of a race distinguished for a rare and detached purity, and of a religion which makes of innocence the Mother of God. In its bodily aspects it became like a war of devils upon angels; as if England could produce nothing but torturers, and Ireland nothing but martyrs. Such was a part of the price paid by the Irish body and the English soul, for the privilege of patching up a Prussian after the sabre-stroke of Jena.

But Germany was not merely present in the spirit: Germany was present in the flesh. Without any desire to underrate the exploits of the English or the Orangemen, I can safely say that the finest touches were added by soldiers trained in a tradition inherited from the horrors of the Thirty Years' War, and of what the old ballad called "the cruel wars of High Germanie." An Irishman I know, whose brother is a soldier, and who has relatives in many distinguished posts of the British army, told me that in his childhood the legend (or rather the truth) of '98 was so frightfully alive that his own mother would not have the word "soldier" spoken in her house. Wherever we thus find the tradition alive we find that the hateful soldier means especially the German soldier. When the Irish say, as some of them do say, that the German mercenary was worse than the Orangemen, they say as much as human mouth can utter. Beyond that there is nothing but the curse of God, which shall be uttered in an unknown tongue.

The practice of using German soldiers, and even whole German regiments, in the make-up of the British army, came in with our German princes, and reappeared on many important occasions in our eighteenth-century history. They were probably among those who encamped triumphantly upon Drumossie Moor, and also (which is a more gratifying thought) among those who ran away with great rapidity at Prestonpans. When that very typical German, George III., narrow, serious, of a stunted culture and coarse in his very domesticity, quarrelled with all that was spirited, not only in the democracy of America but in the aristocracy of England, German troops were very fitted to be his ambassadors beyond the Atlantic. With their well-drilled formations they followed Burgoyne in that woodland march that failed at Saratoga; and with their wooden faces beheld our downfall. Their presence had long had its effect in various ways. In one way, curiously enough, their very militarism helped England to be less military; and especially to be more mercantile. It began to be felt, faintly of course and never consciously, that fighting was a thing that foreigners had to do. It vaguely increased the prestige of the Germans as the military people, to the disadvantage of the French, whom it was the interest of our vanity to underrate. The mere mixture of their uniforms with ours made a background of pageantry in which it seemed more and more natural that English and German potentates should salute each other like cousins, and, in a sense, live in each other's countries. Thus in 1908 the German Emperor was already regarded as something of a menace by the English politicians, and as nothing but a madman by the English people. Yet it did not seem in any way disgusting or dangerous that Edward VII. should appear upon occasion in a Prussian uniform. Edward VII. was himself a friend to France, and worked for the French Alliance. Yet his appearance in the red trousers of a French soldier would have struck many people as funny; as funny as if he had dressed up as a Chinaman.

But the German hirelings or allies had another character

which (by that same strain of evil coincidence which we are tracing in this book) encouraged all that was worst in the English conservatism and inequality, while discouraging all that was best in it. It is true that the ideal Englishman was too much of a squire; but it is just to add that the ideal squire was a good squire. The best squire I know in fiction is Duke Theseus in "The Midsummer Night's Dream," who is kind to his people and proud of his dogs; and would be a perfect human being if he were not just a little bit prone to be kind to both of them in the same way. But such natural and even pagan good-nature is consonant with the warm wet woods and comfortable clouds of South England; it never had any place among the harsh and thrifty squires in the plains of East Prussia, the land of the East Wind. They were peevish as well as proud, and everything they created, but especially their army, was made coherent by sheer brutality. Discipline was cruel enough in all the eighteenth-century armies, created long after the decay of any faith or hope that could hold men together. But the state that was first in Germany was first in ferocity. Frederick the Great had to forbid his English admirers to follow his regiments during the campaign, lest they should discover that the most enlightened of kings had only excluded torture from law to impose it without law. This influence, as we have seen, left on Ireland a fearful mark which will never be effaced. English rule in Ireland had been bad before; but in the broadening light of the revolutionary century I doubt whether it could have continued as bad, if we had not taken a side that forced us to flatter barbarian tyranny in Europe. We should hardly have seen such a nightmare as the Anglicising of Ireland if we had not already seen the Germanising of England. But even in England it was not without its effects; and one of its effects was to rouse a man who is, perhaps, the best English witness to the effect on the England of that time of the Alliance with Germany. With that man I shall deal in the chapter that follows.

CHAPTER V

THE LOST ENGLAND

Telling the truth about Ireland is not very pleasant to a patriotic Englishman; but it is very patriotic. It is the truth and nothing but the truth which I have but touched on in the last chapter. Several times, and especially at the beginning of this war, we narrowly escaped ruin because we neglected that truth, and would insist on treating our crimes of the '98 and after as very distant; while in Irish feeling, and in fact, they are very near. Repentance of this remote sort is not at all appropriate to the case, and will not do. It may be a good thing to forget and forgive; but it is altogether too easy a trick to forget and be forgiven.

The truth about Ireland is simply this: that the relations between England and Ireland are the relations between two men who have to travel together, one of whom tried to stab the other at the last stopping-place or to poison the other at the last inn. Conversation may be courteous, but it will be occasionally forced. The topic of attempted murder, its examples in history and fiction, may be tactfully avoided in the sallies; but it will be occasionally present in the thoughts. Silences, not devoid of strain, will fall from time to time. The partially murdered person may even think an assault unlikely to recur; but it is asking too much, perhaps, to expect him to find it impossible to imagine. And even if, as God grant, the predominant partner is really sorry for his former manner of predominating, and proves it in some unmistakable manner—as by saving the other from robbers at great personal risk—the victim may still be unable to repress an abstract psychological wonder about when his companion first began to feel like that. Now this is not in the least an exaggerated parable of the position of England towards Ireland, not only in '98, but far back from the treason that broke the Treaty of Limerick and far onwards through the Great Famine and after. The conduct of the English towards the Irish after the Rebellion was quite simply the conduct of one man who traps and binds another, and then calmly cuts him about with a knife. The conduct during the Famine was quite simply the conduct of the first man if he entertained the later moments of the second man, by remarking in a chatty manner on the very hopeful chances of his bleeding to death. The British Prime Minister publicly refused to stop the Famine by the use of English ships. The British Prime Minister positively spread the Famine, by making the half-starved populations of Ireland pay for the starved ones. The common verdict of a coroner's jury upon some emaciated wretch was "Wilful murder by Lord John Russell": and that verdict was not only the verdict of Irish public opinion, but is the verdict of history. But there were those in influential positions in England who were not content with publicly approving the act, but publicly proclaimed the motive. The *Times*, which had then a national authority and respectability which gave its words a weight unknown in modern journalism, openly exulted in the prospect of a Golden Age when the kind of Irishman native to Ireland would be "as rare on the banks of the Liffey as a red man on the banks of the Manhattan." It seems sufficiently frantic that such a thing should have been said by one European of another, or even of a Red Indian, if Red Indians had occupied anything like the place of the Irish then and since; if there were to be a Red Indian Lord Chief Justice and a Red Indian Commander-in-Chief, if the Red Indian Party in Congress, containing first-rate orators and fashionable novelists, could have turned Presidents in and out; if half the best troops of the country were trained with the tomahawk and half the best journalism of the capital written in picture-writing, if later, by general consent, the Chief known as Pine in the Twilight, was the best living poet, or the Chief Thin Red Fox, the ablest living dramatist. If that were realised, the English critic probably would not say anything scornful of red men; or certainly would be sorry he said it. But the extraordinary avowal does mark what was most peculiar in the position. This has not been the common case of misgovernment. It is not merely that the institutions we set up were indefensible; though the curious mark of them is that they were literally indefensible; from Wood's Halfpence to the Irish Church Establishment. There can be no more excuse for the method used by Pitt than for the method used by Pigott. But it differs further from ordinary misrule in the vital matter of its object. The coercion was not imposed that the people might live quietly, but that the people might die quietly. And then we sit in an owlish innocence of our sin, and debate whether the Irish might conceivably succeed in saving Ireland. We, as a matter of fact, have not even failed to save Ireland. We have simply failed to destroy her.

It is not possible to reverse this judgment or to take away a single count from it. Is there, then, anything whatever to be said for the English in the matter? There is: though the English never by any chance say it. Nor do the Irish say it; though it is in a sense a weakness as well as a defence. One would think the Irish had reason to say anything that can be said against the English ruling class, but they have not said, indeed they have hardly discovered, one quite simple fact—that it rules England. They are right in asking that the Irish should have a say in the Irish government, but they are quite wrong in supposing that the English have any particular say in English government. And I seriously believe I am not deceived by any national bias, when I say that the common Englishman would be quite incapable of the cruelties that were committed in his name. But, most important of all, it is the historical fact that there was another England, an England consisting of common Englishmen, which not only certainly would have done better, but actually did make some considerable attempt to do better. If anyone asks for the evidence, the answer is that the evidence has been destroyed, or at least deliberately boycotted: but can be found in the unfashionable corners of literature; and, when found, is final. If anyone asks for the great men of such a potential democratic England, the answer is that the great men are labelled small men, or not labelled at all; have been successfully belittled as the emancipation of which they dreamed has dwindled. The greatest of them is now little more than a name; he is criticised to be underrated and not to be understood; but he presented all that alternative and more liberal Englishry; and was enormously popular because he presented it. In taking him as the type of it we may tell most shortly the whole of this forgotten tale. And, even when I begin to tell it, I find myself in the presence of that ubiquitous evil which is the subject of this book. It is a fact, and I think it is not a coincidence, that in standing for a moment where this Englishman stood, I again find myself confronted by the German soldier.

The son of a small Surrey farmer, a respectable Tory and churchman, ventured to plead against certain extraordinary cruelties being inflicted on Englishmen whose hands were tied, by the whips of German superiors; who were then parading in English fields their stiff foreign uniforms and their sanguinary foreign discipline. In the countries from which they came, of course, such torments were the one monotonous means of driving men on to perish in the dead dynastic quarrels of the north; but to poor Will Cobbett, in his provincial island, knowing little but the low hills and hedges around the little church where he now lies buried, the incident seemed odd—nay, unpleasing. He knew, of course, that there was then flogging in the British army also; but the German standard was notoriously severe in such things, and was something of an acquired taste. Added to which he had all sorts of old grandmotherly prejudices about Englishmen being punished by Englishmen, and notions of that sort. He protested, not only in speech, but actually in print. He was soon made to learn the perils of meddling in the high politics of the High Dutch militarists. The fine feelings of the foreign mercenaries were soothed by Cobbett being flung into Newgate for two years and beggared by a fine of £1000. That small incident is a small transparent picture of the Holy Alliance; of what was really meant by a country, once half liberalised, taking up the cause of the foreign kings. This, and not "The Meeting of Wellington and Blucher," should be engraved as the great scene of the war. From this intemperate Fenians should learn that the Teutonic mercenaries did not confine themselves solely to torturing Irishmen. They were equally ready to torture Englishmen: for mercenaries are mostly unprejudiced. To Cobbett's eye we were suffering from allies exactly as we should suffer from invaders. Boney was a bogey; but the German was a nightmare, a thing actually sitting on top of us. In Ireland the Alliance meant the ruin of anything and everything Irish, from the creed of St. Patrick to the mere colour green. But in England also it meant the ruin of anything and everything English, from the Habeas Corpus Act to Cobbett.

After this affair of the scourging, he wielded his pen like a scourge until he died. This terrible pamphleteer was one of those men who exist to prove the distinction between a biography and a life. From his biographies you will learn that he was a Radical who had once been a Tory. From his life, if there were one, you would learn that he was always a Radical because he was always a Tory. Few men changed less; it was round him that the politicians like Pitt chopped and changed, like fakirs dancing round a sacred rock. His secret is buried with him; it is that he really cared about the English people. He was conservative because he cared for their past, and liberal because he cared for their future. But he was much more than this. He had two forms of moral manhood very rare in our time: he was ready to uproot ancient successes, and he was ready to defy oncoming doom. Burke said that few are the partisans of a tyranny that has departed: he might have added that fewer still are the critics of a tyranny that has remained. Burke certainly was not one of them. While lashing himself into a lunacy against the French Revolution, which only very incidentally destroyed the property of the rich, he never criticised (to do him justice, perhaps never saw) the English Revolution, which began with the sack of convents, and ended with the fencing in of enclosures; a revolution which sweepingly and systematically destroyed the property of the poor. While rhetorically putting the Englishman in a castle, politically he would not allow him on a common. Cobbett, a much more historical thinker, saw the beginning of Capitalism in the Tudor pillage and deplored it; he saw the triumph of Capitalism in the industrial cities and defied it. The paradox he was maintaining really amounted to the assertion that Westminster Abbey is rather more national than Welbeck Abbey. The same paradox would have led him to maintain that a Warwickshire man had more reason to be proud of Stratford-on-Avon than of Birmingham. He would no more have thought of looking for England in Birmingham than of looking for Ireland in Belfast.

The prestige of Cobbett's excellent literary style has survived the persecution of his equally excellent opinions. But that style also is underrated through the loss of the real English tradition. More cautious schools have missed the fact that the very genius of the English tongue tends not only to vigour, but specially to violence. The Englishman of the leading articles is calm, moderate, and restrained; but then the Englishman of the leading articles is a Prussian. The mere English consonants are full of Cobbett. Dr. Johnson was our great man of letters when he said "stinks," not when he said "putrefaction." Take some common phrase like "raining cats and dogs," and note not only the extravagance of imagery (though that is very Shakespearean), but a jagged energy in the very spelling. Say "chats" and "chiens" and it is not the same. Perhaps the old national genius has survived the urban enslavement most spiritedly in our comic songs, admired by all men of travel and continental culture, by Mr. George Moore as by Mr. Belloc. One (to which I am much attached) had a chorus—

"O wind from the South
Blow mud in the mouth
Of Jane, Jane, Jane."

Note, again, not only the tremendous vision of clinging soils carried skywards in the tornado, but also the suitability of the mere sounds. Say "bone" and "bouche" for mud and mouth and it is not the same. Cobbett was a wind from the South; and if he occasionally seemed to stop his enemies' mouths with mud, it was the real soil of South England.

And as his seemingly mad language is very literary, so his seemingly mad meaning is very historical. Modern people do not understand him because they do not understand the difference between exaggerating a truth and exaggerating a lie. He did exaggerate, but what he knew, not what he did not know. He only appears paradoxical because he upheld tradition against fashion. A paradox is a fantastic thing that is said once: a fashion is a more fantastic thing that is said a sufficient number of times. I could give numberless examples in Cobbett's case, but I will give only one. Anyone who finds himself full in the central path of Cobbett's fury sometimes has something like a physical shock. No one who has read "The History of the Reformation" will ever forget the passage (I forget the precise words) in which he says the mere thought of such a person as Cranmer makes the brain reel, and, for an instant, doubt the goodness of God; but that peace and faith flow back into the soul when we remember that he was burned alive. Now this is extravagant. It takes the breath away; and it was meant to. But what I wish to point out is that a much more extravagant view of Cranmer was, in Cobbett's day, the accepted view of Cranmer; not as a momentary image, but as an immovable historical monument. Thousands of parsons and penmen dutifully set down Cranmer among the saints and martyrs; and there are many respectable people who would do so still. This is not an exaggerated truth, but an established lie. Cranmer was not such a monstrosity of meanness as Cobbett implies; but he was mean. But there is no question of his being less saintly than the parsonage believed; he was not a saint at all; and not very attractive even as a sinner. He was no more a martyr for being burned than Crippen for being hanged.

Cobbett was defeated because the English people was defeated. After the frame-breaking riots, men, as men, were beaten: and machines, as machines, had beaten them. Peterloo was as much the defeat of the English as Waterloo was the defeat of the French. Ireland did not get Home Rule because England did not get it. Cobbett would not forcibly incorporate Ireland, least of all the corpse of Ireland. But before his defeat Cobbett had an enormous following; his "Register" was what the serial novels of Dickens were afterwards to be. Dickens, by the way, inherited the same instinct for abrupt diction, and probably enjoyed writing "gas and gaiters" more than any two other words in his works. But Dickens was narrower than Cobbett, not by any fault of his own, but because in the intervening epoch of the triumph of Scrooge and Gradgrind the link with our Christian past had been lost, save in the single matter of Christmas, which Dickens rescued romantically and by a hair's-breadth escape. Cobbett was a yeoman; that is, a man free and farming a small estate. By Dickens's time, yeomen seemed as antiquated as bowmen. Cobbett was mediaeval; that is, he was in almost every way the opposite of what that word means to-day. He was as egalitarian as St. Francis, and as independent as Robin Hood. Like that other yeoman in the ballad, he bore in hand a mighty bow; what some of his enemies would have called a long bow. But though he sometimes overshot the mark of truth, he never shot away from it, like Froude. His account of that sixteenth century in which the mediaeval civilisation ended, is not more and not less picturesque than Froude's: the difference is in the dull detail of truth. That crisis was *not* the foundling of a strong Tudor monarchy, for the monarchy almost immediately perished; it *was* the founding of a strong class holding all the capital and land, for it holds them to this day. Cobbett would have asked nothing better than to bend his mediaeval bow to the cry of "St. George for Merry England," for though he pointed to the other and uglier side of the Waterloo medal, he was patriotic; and his premonitions were rather against Blucher than Wellington. But if we take that old war-cry as his final word (and he would have accepted it) we must note how every term in it points away from what the modern plutocrats call either progress or empire. It involves the invocation of saints, the most popular and the most forbidden form of mediævalism. The modern Imperialist no more thinks of St. George in England than he thinks of St. John in St. John's Wood. It is nationalist in the narrowest sense; and no one knows the beauty and simplicity of the Middle Ages who has not seen St. George's Cross separate, as it was at Creçy or Flodden, and noticed how much finer a flag it is than the Union Jack. And the word "merry" bears witness to an England famous for its music and dancing before the coming of the Puritans, the last traces of which have been stamped out by a social discipline utterly un-English. Not for two years, but for ten decades Cobbett has been in prison; and his enemy, the "efficient" foreigner, has walked about in the sunlight, magnificent, and a model for men. I do not think that even the Prussians ever boasted about "Merry Prussia."

CHAPTER VI

HAMLET AND THE DANES

In the one classic and perfect literary product that ever came out of Germany—I do not mean "Faust," but Grimm's Fairy Tales—there is a gorgeous story about a boy who went through a number of experiences without learning how to shudder. In one of them, I remember, he was sitting by the fireside and a pair of live legs fell down the chimney and walked about the room by themselves. Afterwards the rest fell down and joined up; but this was almost an anti-climax. Now that is very charming, and full of the best German domesticity. It suggests truly what wild adventures the traveller can find by stopping at home. But it also illustrates in various ways how that great German influence on England, which is the matter of these essays, began in good things and gradually turned to bad. It began as a literary influence, in the lurid tales of Hoffmann, the tale of "Sintram," and so on; the revisualising of the dark background of forest behind our European cities. That old German darkness was immeasurably livelier than the new German light. The devils of Germany were much better than the angels. Look at the Teutonic pictures of "The Three Huntsmen" and observe that while the wicked huntsman is effective in his own way, the good huntsman is weak in every way, a sort of sexless woman with a face like a teaspoon. But there is more in these first forest tales, these homely horrors. In the earlier stages they have exactly this salt of salvation, that the boy does *not* shudder. They are made fearful that he may be fearless, not that he may fear. As long as that limit is kept, the barbaric dreamland is decent; and though individuals like Coleridge and De Quincey mixed it with worse things (such as opium), they kept that romantic rudiment upon the whole. But the one disadvantage of a forest is that one may lose one's way in it. And the one danger is not that we may meet devils, but that we may worship them. In other words, the danger is one always associated, by the instinct of folk-lore, with forests; it is *enchantment,* or the fixed loss of oneself in some unnatural captivity or spiritual servitude. And in the evolution of Germanism, from Hoffmann to Hauptmann, we do see this growing tendency to take horror seriously, which is diabolism. The German begins to have an eerie abstract sympathy with the force and fear he describes, as distinct from their objective. The German is no longer sympathising with the boy against the goblin, but rather with the goblin against the boy. There goes with it, as always goes with idolatry, a dehumanised seriousness; the men of the forest are already building upon a mountain the empty throne of the Superman. Now it is just at this point that I for one, and most men who love truth as well as tales, begin to lose interest. I am all for "going out into the world to seek my fortune," but I do not want to find it—and find it is only being chained for ever among the frozen figures of the Sieges Allees. I do not want to be an idolator, still less an idol. I am all for going to fairyland, but I am also all for coming back. That is, I will admire, but I will not be magnetised, either by mysticism or militarism. I am all for German fantasy, but I will resist German earnestness till I die. I am all for Grimm's Fairy Tales; but if there is such a thing as Grimm's Law, I would break it, if I knew what it was. I like the Prussian's legs (in their beautiful boots) to fall down the chimney and walk about my room. But when he procures a head and begins to talk, I feel a little bored. The Germans cannot really be deep because they will not consent to be superficial. They are bewitched by art, and stare at it, and cannot see round it. They will not believe that art is a light and slight thing—a feather, even if it be from an angelic wing. Only the slime is at the bottom of a pool; the sky is on the surface.

We see this in that very typical process, the Germanising of Shakespeare. I do not complain of the Germans forgetting that Shakespeare was an Englishman. I complain of their forgetting that Shakespeare was a man; that he had moods, that he made mistakes, and, above all, that he knew his art was an art and not an attribute of deity. That is what is the matter with the Germans; they cannot "ring fancy's knell"; their knells have no gaiety. The phrase of Hamlet about "holding the mirror up to nature" is always quoted by such earnest critics as meaning that art is nothing if not realistic. But it really means (or at least its author really thought) that art is nothing if not artificial. Realists, like other barbarians, really *believe* the mirror; and therefore break the mirror. Also they leave out the phrase "as 'twere," which must be read into every remark of Shakespeare, and especially every remark of Hamlet. What I mean by believing the mirror, and breaking it, can be recorded in one case I remember; in which a realistic critic quoted German authorities to prove that Hamlet had a particular psycho-pathological abnormality, which is admittedly nowhere mentioned in the play. The critic was bewitched; he was thinking of Hamlet as a real man, with a background behind him three dimensions deep—which does not exist in a looking-glass. "The best in this kind are but shadows." No German commentator has ever made an adequate note on that. Nevertheless, Shakespeare was an Englishman; he was nowhere more English than in his blunders; but he was nowhere more successful than in the description of very English types of character. And if anything is to be said about Hamlet, beyond what Shakespeare has said about him, I should say that Hamlet was an Englishman too. He was as much an Englishman as he was a gentleman, and he had the very grave weaknesses of both characters. The chief English fault, especially in the nineteenth century, has been lack of decision, not only lack of decision in action, but lack of the equally essential decision in thought—which some call dogma. And in the politics of the last century, this English Hamlet, as we shall see, played a great part, or rather refused to play it.

There were, then, two elements in the German influence; a sort of pretty playing with terror and a solemn recognition of terrorism. The first pointed to elfland, and the second to—shall we say, Prussia. And by that unconscious symbolism with which all this story develops, it was soon to be dramatically tested, by a definite political query, whether what we really respected was the Teutonic fantasy or the Teutonic fear.

The Germanisation of England, its transition and turning-point, was well typified by the genius of Carlyle. The original charm of Germany had been the charm of the child. The Teutons were never so great as when they were childish; in their religious art and popular imagery the Christ-Child is really a child, though the Christ is hardly a man. The self-conscious fuss of their pedagogy is half-redeemed by the unconscious grace which called a school not a seed-plot of citizens, but merely a garden of children. All the first and best forest-spirit is infancy, its wonder, its wilfulness, even its still innocent fear. Carlyle marks exactly the moment when the German child becomes the spoilt child. The wonder turns to mere mysticism; and mere mysticism always turns to mere immoralism. The wilfulness is no longer liked, but is actually obeyed. The fear becomes a philosophy. Panic hardens into pessimism; or else, what is often equally depressing, optimism.

Carlyle, the most influential English writer of that time, marks all this by the mental interval between his "French Revolution" and his "Frederick the Great." In both he was Germanic. Carlyle was really as sentimental as Goethe; and Goethe was really as sentimental as Werther. Carlyle understood everything about the French Revolution, except that it was a French revolution. He could not conceive that cold anger that comes from a love of insulted truth. It seemed to him absurd that a man should die, or do murder, for the First Proposition of Euclid; should relish an egalitarian state like an equilateral triangle; or should defend the Pons Asinorum as Codes defended the Tiber bridge.

But anyone who does not understand that does not understand the French Revolution—nor, for that matter, the American Revolution. "We hold these truths to be self-evident": it was the fanaticism of truism. But though Carlyle had no real respect for liberty, he had a real reverence for anarchy. He admired elemental energy. The violence which repelled most men from the Revolution was the one thing that attracted him to it. While a Whig like Macaulay respected the Girondists but deplored the Mountain, a Tory like Carlyle rather liked the Mountain and quite unduly despised the Girondists. This appetite for formless force belongs, of course, to the forests, to Germany. But when Carlyle got there, there fell upon him a sort of spell which is his tragedy and the English tragedy, and, in no small degree, the German tragedy too. The real romance of the Teutons was largely a romance of the Southern Teutons, with their castles, which are almost literally castles in the air, and their river which is walled with vineyards and rhymes so naturally to wine. But as Carlyle's was rootedly a romance of conquest, he had to prove that the thing which conquered in Germany was really more poetical than anything else in Germany. Now the thing that conquered in Germany was about the most prosaic thing of which the world ever grew weary. There is a great deal more poetry in Brixton than in Berlin. Stella said that Swift could write charmingly about a broom-stick; and poor Carlyle had to write romantically about a ramrod. Compare him with Heine, who had also a detached taste in the mystical grotesques of Germany, but who saw what was their enemy: and offered to nail up the Prussian eagle like an old crow as a target for the archers of the Rhine. Its prosaic essence is not proved by the fact that it did not produce poets: it is proved by the more deadly fact that it did. The actual written poetry of Frederick the Great, for instance, was not even German or barbaric, but simply feeble—and French. Thus Carlyle became continually gloomier as his fit of the blues deepened into Prussian blues; nor can there be any wonder. His philosophy had brought out the result that the Prussian was the first of Germans, and, therefore, the first of men. No wonder he looked at the rest of us with little hope.

But a stronger test was coming both for Carlyle and England. Prussia, plodding, policing, as materialist as mud, went on solidifying and strengthening after unconquered Russia and unconquered England had rescued her where she lay prostrate under Napoleon. In this interval the two most important events were the Polish national revival, with which Russia was half inclined to be sympathetic, but Prussia was implacably coercionist; and the positive refusal of the crown of a united Germany by the King of Prussia, simply because it was constitutionally offered by a free German Convention. Prussia did not want to lead the Germans: she wanted to conquer the Germans. And she wanted to conquer other people first. She had already found her brutal, if humorous, embodiment in Bismarck; and he began with a scheme full of brutality and not without humour. He took up, or rather pretended to take up, the claim of the Prince of Augustenberg to duchies which were a quite lawful part of the land of Denmark. In support of this small pretender he enlisted two large things, the Germanic body called the Bund and the Austrian Empire. It is possibly needless to say that after he had seized the disputed provinces by pure Prussian violence, he kicked out the Prince of Augustenberg, kicked out the German Bund, and finally kicked out the Austrian Empire too, in the sudden campaign of Sadowa. He was a good husband and a good father; he did not paint in water colours; and of such is the Kingdom of Heaven. But the symbolic intensity of the incident was this. The Danes expected protection from England; and if there had been any sincerity in the ideal side of our Teutonism they ought to have had it. They ought to have had it even by the pedantries of the time, which already talked of Latin inferiority: and were never weary of explaining that the country of Richelieu could not rule and the country of Napoleon could not fight. But if it was necessary for whosoever would be saved to be a Teuton, the Danes were more Teuton than the Prussians. If it be a matter of vital importance to be descended from Vikings, the Danes really were descended from Vikings, while the Prussians were descended from mongrel Slavonic savages. If Protestantism be progress, the Danes were Protestant; while they had attained quite peculiar success and wealth in that small ownership and intensive cultivation which is very commonly a boast of Catholic lands. They had in a quite arresting degree what was claimed for the Germanics as against Latin revolutionism: quiet freedom, quiet prosperity, a simple love of fields and of the sea. But, moreover, by that coincidence which dogs this drama, the English of that Victorian epoch had found their freshest impression of the northern spirit of infancy and wonder in the works of a Danish man of genius, whose stories and sketches were so popular in England as almost to have become English. Good as Grimm's Fairy Tales were, they had been collected and not created by the modern German; they were a museum of things older than any nation, of the dateless age of once-upon-a-time. When the English romantics wanted to find the folk-tale spirit still alive, they found it in the small country of one of those small kings, with whom the folk-tales are almost comically crowded. There they found what we call an original writer, who was nevertheless the image of the origins. They found a whole fairyland in one head and under one nineteenth-century top hat. Those of the English who were then children owe to Hans Andersen more than to any of their own writers, that essential educational emotion which feels that domesticity is not dull but rather fantastic; that sense of the fairyland of furniture, and the travel and adventure of the farmyard. His treatment of inanimate things as animate was not a cold and awkward allegory: it was a true sense of a dumb divinity in things that are. Through him a child did feel that the chair he sat on was something like a wooden horse. Through him children and the happier kind of men did feel

58

themselves covered by a roof as by the folded wings of some vast domestic fowl; and feel common doors like great mouths that opened to utter welcome. In the story of "The Fir Tree" he transplanted to England a living bush that can still blossom into candles. And in his tale of "The Tin Soldier" he uttered the true defence of romantic militarism against the prigs who would forbid it even as a toy for the nursery. He suggested, in the true tradition of the folk-tales, that the dignity of the fighter is not in his largeness but rather in his smallness, in his stiff loyalty and heroic helplessness in the hands of larger and lower things. These things, alas, were an allegory. When Prussia, finding her crimes unpunished, afterwards carried them into France as well as Denmark, Carlyle and his school made some effort to justify their Germanism, by pitting what they called the piety and simplicity of Germany against what they called the cynicism and ribaldry of France. But nobody could possibly pretend that Bismarck was more pious and simple than Hans Andersen; yet the Carlyleans looked on with silence or approval while the innocent toy kingdom was broken like a toy. Here again, it is enormously probable that England would have struck upon the right side, if the English people had been the English Government. Among other coincidences, the Danish princess who had married the English heir was something very like a fairy princess to the English crowd. The national poet had hailed her as a daughter of the sea-kings; and she was, and indeed still is, the most popular royal figure in England. But whatever our people may have been like, our politicians were on the very tamest level of timidity and the fear of force to which they have ever sunk. The Tin Soldier of the Danish army and the paper boat of the Danish navy, as in the story, were swept away down the great gutter, down that colossal *cloaca* that leads to the vast cesspool of Berlin.

Why, as a fact, did not England interpose? There were a great many reasons given, but I think they were all various inferences from one reason; indirect results and sometimes quite illogical results, of what we have called the Germanisation of England. First, the very insularity on which we insisted was barbaric, in its refusal of a seat in the central senate of the nations. What we called our splendid isolation became a rather ignominious sleeping-partnership with Prussia. Next, we were largely trained in irresponsibility by our contemporary historians, Freeman and Green, teaching us to be proud of a possible descent from King Arthur's nameless enemies and not from King Arthur. King Arthur might not be historical, but at least he was legendary. Hengist and Horsa were not even legendary, for they left no legend. Anybody could see what was obligatory on the representative of Arthur; he was bound to be chivalrous, that is, to be European. But nobody could imagine what was obligatory on the representative of Horsa, unless it were to be horsy. That was perhaps the only part of the Anglo-Saxon programme that the contemporary English really carried out. Then, in the very real decline from Cobbett to Cobden (that is, from a broad to a narrow manliness and good sense) there had grown up the cult of a very curious kind of peace, to be spread all over the world not by pilgrims, but by pedlars. Mystics from the beginning had made vows of peace—but they added to them vows of poverty. Vows of poverty were not in the Cobdenite's line. Then, again, there was the positive praise of Prussia, to which steadily worsening case the Carlyleans were already committed. But beyond these, there was something else, a spirit which had more infected us as a whole. That spirit was the spirit of Hamlet. We gave the grand name of "evolution" to a notion that things do themselves. Our wealth, our insularity, our gradual loss of faith, had so dazed us that the old Christian England haunted us like a ghost in whom we could not quite believe. An aristocrat like Palmerston, loving freedom and hating the upstart despotism, must have looked on at its cold brutality not without that ugly question which Hamlet asked himself—am I a coward?

It cannot be
But I am pigeon-livered and lack gall
To make oppression bitter; or 'ere this
I should have fatted all the region kites
With this slave's offal.

We made dumb our anger and our honour; but it has not brought us peace.

CHAPTER VII

_____

THE MIDNIGHT OF EUROPE

Among the minor crimes of England may be classed the shallow criticism and easy abandonment of Napoleon III. The Victorian English had a very bad habit of being influenced by words and at the same time pretending to despise them. They would build their whole historical philosophy upon two or three titles, and then refuse to get even the titles right. The solid Victorian Englishman, with his whiskers and his Parliamentary vote, was quite content to say that Louis Napoleon and William of Prussia both became Emperors—by which he meant autocrats. His whiskers would have bristled with rage and he would have stormed at you for hair-splitting and "lingo," if you had answered that William was German Emperor, while Napoleon was not French Emperor, but only Emperor of the French. What could such mere order of the words matter? Yet the same Victorian would have been even more indignant if he had been asked to be satisfied with an Art Master, when he had advertised for a Master of Arts. His irritation would have increased if the Art Master had promised him a sea-piece and had brought him a piece of the sea; or if, during the decoration of his house, the same aesthetic humourist had undertaken to procure some Indian Red and had produced a Red Indian.

The Englishman would not see that if there was only a verbal difference between the French Emperor and the Emperor of the French, so, if it came to that, it was a verbal difference between the Emperor and the Republic, or even between a Parliament and no Parliament. For him an Emperor meant merely despotism; he had not yet learned that a Parliament may mean merely oligarchy. He did not know that the English people would soon be made impotent, not by the disfranchising of their constituents, but simply by the silencing of their members; and that the governing class of England did not now depend upon rotten boroughs, but upon rotten representatives. Therefore he did not understand Bonapartism. He did not understand that French democracy became more democratic, not less, when it turned all France into one constituency which elected one member. He did not understand that many dragged down the Republic because it was not republican, but purely senatorial. He was yet to learn how quite corruptly senatorial a great representative assembly can become. Yet in England to-day we hear "the decline of Parliament" talked about and taken for granted by the best Parliamentarians—Mr. Balfour, for instance—and we hear the one partly French and wholly Jacobin historian of the French Revolution recommending for the English evil a revival of the power of the Crown. It seems that so far from having left Louis Napoleon far behind in the grey dust of the dead despotisms, it is not at all improbable that our most extreme revolutionary developments may end where Louis Napoleon began.

In other words, the Victorian Englishman did not understand the words "Emperor of the French." The type of title was deliberately chosen to express the idea of an elective and popular origin; as against such a phrase as "the German Emperor," which expresses an almost transcendental tribal patriarchate, or such a phrase as "King of Prussia," which suggests personal ownership of a whole territory. To treat the *Coup d'état* as unpardonable is to justify riot against despotism, but forbid any riot against aristocracy. Yet the idea expressed in "The Emperor of the French" is not dead, but rather risen from the dead. It is the idea that while a government may pretend to be a popular government, only a person can be really popular. Indeed, the idea is still the crown of American democracy, as it was for a time the crown of French democracy. The very powerful official who makes the choice of that great people for peace or war, might very well be called, not the President of the United States, but the President of the Americans. In Italy we have seen the King and the mob prevail over the conservatism of the Parliament, and in Russia the new popular policy sacramentally symbolised by the Czar riding at the head of the new armies. But in one place, at least, the actual form of words exists; and the actual form of words has been splendidly justified. One man among the sons of men has been permitted to fulfil a courtly formula with awful and disastrous fidelity. Political and geographical ruin have written one last royal title across the sky; the loss of palace and capital and territory have but isolated and made evident the people that has not been lost; not laws but the love of exiles, not soil but the souls of men, still make certain that five true words shall yet be written in the corrupt and fanciful chronicles of mankind: "The King of the Belgians."

It is a common phrase, recurring constantly in the real if rabid eloquence of Victor Hugo, that Napoleon III. was a mere ape of Napoleon I. That is, that he had, as the politician says, in "L'Aiglon," "le petit chapeau, mais pas la tête"; that he was merely a bad imitation. This is extravagantly exaggerative; and those who say it, moreover, often miss the two or three points of resemblance which really exist in the exaggeration. One resemblance there certainly was. In both Napoleons it has been suggested that the glory was not so great as it seemed; but in both it can be emphatically added that the eclipse was not so great as it seemed either. Both succeeded at first and failed at last. But both succeeded at last, even after the failure. If at this moment we owe thanks to Napoleon Bonaparte for the armies of united France, we also owe some thanks to Louis Bonaparte for the armies of united Italy. That great movement to a freer and more chivalrous Europe which we call to-day the Cause of the Allies, had its forerunners and first victories before our time; and it not only won at Arcola, but also at Solferino. Men who remembered

64

Louis Napoleon when he mooned about the Blessington *salon*, and was supposed to be almost mentally deficient, used to say he deceived Europe twice; once when he made men think him an imbecile, and once when he made them think him a statesman. But he deceived them a third time; when he made them think he was dead; and had done nothing.

In spite of the unbridled verse of Hugo and the even more unbridled prose of Kinglake, Napoleon III. is really and solely discredited in history because of the catastrophe of 1870. Hugo hurled any amount of lightning on Louis Napoleon; but he threw very little light on him. Some passages in the "Châtiments" are really caricatures carved in eternal marble. They will always be valuable in reminding generations too vague and soft, as were the Victorians, of the great truth that hatred is beautiful, when it is hatred of the ugliness of the soul. But most of them could have been written about Haman, or Heliogabalus, or King John, or Queen Elizabeth, as much as about poor Louis Napoleon; they bear no trace of any comprehension of his quite interesting aims, and his quite comprehensible contempt for the fat-souled senatorial politicians. And if a real revolutionist like Hugo did not do justice to the revolutionary element in Cæsarism, it need hardly be said that a rather Primrose League Tory like Tennyson did not. Kinglake's curiously acrid insistence upon the *Coup d'état* is, I fear, only an indulgence in one of the least pleasing pleasures of our national pen and press, and one which afterwards altogether ran away with us over the Dreyfus case. It is an unfortunate habit of publicly repenting for other people's sins. If this came easy to an Englishman like Kinglake, it came, of course, still easier to a German like Queen Victoria's husband and even to Queen Victoria herself, who was naturally influenced by him. But in so far as the sensible masses of the English nation took any interest in the matter, it is probable that they sympathised with Palmerston, who was as popular as the Prince Consort was unpopular. The black mark against Louis Napoleon's name until now, has simply been Sedan; and it is our whole purpose to-day to turn Sedan into an interlude. If it is not an interlude, it will be the end of the world. But we have sworn to make an end of that ending: warring on until, if only by a purgatory of the nations and the mountainous annihilation of men, the story of the world ends well.

There are, as it were, valleys of history quite close to us, but hidden by the closer hills. One, as we have seen, is that fold in the soft Surrey hills where Cobbett sleeps with his still-born English Revolution. Another is under that height called The Spy of Italy, where a new Napoleon brought back the golden eagles against the black eagles of Austria. Yet that French adventure in support of the Italian insurrection was very important; we are only beginning to understand its importance. It was a defiance to the German Reaction and 1870 was a sort of revenge for it, just as the Balkan victory was a defiance to the German Reaction and 1914 was the attempted revenge for it. It is true that the French liberation of Italy was incomplete, the problem of the Papal States, for instance, being untouched by the Peace of Villafranca. The volcanic but fruitful spirit of Italy had already produced that wonderful, wandering, and almost omnipresent personality whose red shirt was to be a walking flag: Garibaldi. And many English Liberals sympathised with him and his extremists as against the peace. Palmerston called it "the peace that passeth all understanding": but the profanity of that hilarious old heathen was nearer the mark than he knew: there were really present some of those deep things which he did not understand. To quarrel with the Pope, but to compromise with him, was an instinct with the Bonapartes; an instinct no Anglo-Saxon could be expected to understand. They knew the truth; that Anti-Clericalism is not a Protestant movement, but a Catholic mood. And after all the English Liberals could not get their own Government to risk what the French Government had risked; and Napoleon III. might well have retorted on Palmerston, his rival in international Liberalism, that half a war was better than no fighting. Swinburne called Villafranca "The

Halt before Rome," and expressed a rhythmic impatience for the time when the world

"Shall ring to the roar of the lion
Proclaiming Republican Rome."

But he might have remembered, after all, that it was not the British lion, that a British poet should have the right to say so imperiously, "Let him roar again. Let him roar again."

It is true that there was no clear call to England from Italy, as there certainly was from Denmark. The great powers were not bound to help Italy to become a nation, as they were bound to support the unquestioned fact that Denmark was one. Indeed the great Italian patriot was to experience both extremes of the English paradox, and, curiously enough, in connection with both the two national and anti-German causes. For Italy he gained the support of the English, but not the support of England. Not a few of our countrymen followed the red shirt; but not in the red coat. And when he came to England, not to plead the cause of Italy but the cause of Denmark, the Italian found he was more popular with the English than any Englishman. He made his way through a forest of salutations, which would willingly have turned itself into a forest of swords. But those who kept the sword kept it sheathed. For the ruling class the valour of the Italian hero, like the beauty of the Danish Princess, was a thing to be admired, that is enjoyed, like a novel—or a newspaper. Palmerston was the very type of Pacifism, because he was the very type of Jingoism. In spirit as restless as Garibaldi, he was in practice as cautious as Cobden. England had the most prudent aristocracy, but the most reckless democracy in the world. It was, and is, the English contradiction, which has so much misrepresented us, especially to the Irish. Our national captains were carpet knights; our knights errant were among the dismounted rabble. When an Austrian general who had flogged women in the conquered provinces appeared in

67

the London streets, some common draymen off a cart behaved with the direct quixotry of Sir Lancelot or Sir Galahad. He had beaten women and they beat him. They regarded themselves simply as avengers of ladies in distress, breaking the bloody whip of a German bully; just as Cobbett had sought to break it when it was wielded over the men of England. The boorishness was in the Germanic or half-Germanic rulers who wore crosses and spurs: the gallantry was in the gutter. English draymen had more chivalry than Teuton aristocrats—or English ones.

I have dwelt a little on this Italian experiment because it lights up Louis Napoleon as what he really was before the eclipse, a politician—perhaps an unscrupulous politician— but certainly a democratic politician. A power seldom falls being wholly faultless; and it is true that the Second Empire became contaminated with cosmopolitan spies and swindlers, justly reviled by such democrats as Rochefort as well as Hugo. But there was no French inefficiency that weighed a hair in the balance compared with the huge and hostile efficiency of Prussia; the tall machine that had struck down Denmark and Austria, and now stood ready to strike again, extinguishing the lamp of the world. There was a hitch before the hammer stroke, and Bismarck adjusted it, as with his finger, by a forgery—for he had many minor accomplishments. France fell: and what fell with her was freedom, and what reigned in her stead only tyrants and the ancient terror. The crowning of the first modern Kaiser in the very palace of the old French kings was an allegory; like an allegory on those Versailles walls. For it was at once the lifting of the old despotic diadem and its descent on the low brow of a barbarian. Louis XI. had returned, and not Louis IX.; and Europe was to know that sceptre on which there is no dove.

The instant evidence that Europe was in the grip of the savage was as simple as it was sinister. The invaders behaved with an innocent impiety and bestiality that had never been known in those lands since Clovis was signed with the cross. To the naked pride of the new men nations simply were not. The struggling populations of two vast provinces were simply carried away like slaves into captivity, as after the sacking of some prehistoric town. France was fined for having pretended to be a nation; and the fine was planned to ruin her forever. Under the pressure of such impossible injustice France cried out to the Christian nations, one after another, and by name. Her last cry ended in a stillness like that which had encircled Denmark.

One man answered; one who had quarrelled with the French and their Emperor; but who knew it was not an emperor that had fallen. Garibaldi, not always wise but to his end a hero, took his station, sword in hand, under the darkening sky of Christendom, and shared the last fate of France. A curious record remains, in which a German commander testifies to the energy and effect of the last strokes of the wounded lion of Aspromonte. But England went away sorrowful, for she had great possessions.

CHAPTER VIII

THE WRONG HORSE

In another chapter I mentioned some of the late Lord Salisbury's remarks with regret, but I trust with respect; for in certain matters he deserved all the respect that can be given to him. His critics said that he "thought aloud"; which is perhaps the noblest thing that can be said of a man. He was jeered at for it by journalists and politicians who had not the capacity to think or the courage to tell their thoughts. And he had one yet finer quality which redeems a hundred lapses of anarchic cynicism. He could change his mind upon the platform: he could repent in public. He could not only think aloud; he could "think better" aloud. And one of the turning-points of Europe had come in the hour when he avowed his conversion from the un-Christian and un-European policy into which his dexterous Oriental master, Disraeli, had dragged him; and declared that England had "put her money on the wrong horse." When he said it, he referred to the backing we gave to the Turk under a fallacious fear of Russia. But I cannot but think that if he had lived much longer, he would have come to feel the same disgust for his long diplomatic support of the Turk's great ally in the North. He did not live, as we have lived, to feel that horse run away with us, and rush on through wilder and wilder places, until we knew that we were riding on the nightmare.

What was this thing to which we trusted? And how may we most quickly explain its development from a dream to a nightmare, and the hair's-breadth escape by which it did not hurl us to destruction, as it seems to be hurling the Turk? It is a certain spirit; and we must not ask for too logical a definition of it, for the people whom it possesses disown logic; and the whole thing is not so much a theory as a confusion of thought. Its widest and most elementary character is adumbrated in the word Teutonism or Pan-Germanism; and with this (which was what appeared to win in 1870) we had better begin. The nature of Pan-Germanism may be allegorised and abbreviated somewhat thus:

The horse asserts that all other creatures are morally bound to sacrifice their interests to his, on the specific ground that he possesses all noble and necessary qualities, and is an end in himself. It is pointed out in answer that when climbing a tree the horse is less graceful than the cat; that lovers and poets seldom urge the horse to make a noise all night like the nightingale; that when submerged for some long time under water, he is less happy than the haddock; and that when he is cut open pearls are less often found in him than in an oyster. He is not content to answer (though, being a muddle-headed horse, he does use this answer also) that having an undivided hoof is more than pearls or oceans or all ascension or song. He reflects for a few years on the subject of cats; and at last discovers in the cat "the characteristic equine quality of caudality, or a tail"; so that cats *are* horses, and wave on every tree-top the tail which is the equine banner. Nightingales are found to have legs, which explains their power of song. Haddocks are vertebrates; and therefore are sea-horses. And though the oyster outwardly presents dissimilarities which seem to divide him from the horse, he is by the all-filling nature-might of the same horse-moving energy sustained.

Now this horse is intellectually the wrong horse. It is not perhaps going too far to say that this horse is a donkey. For it is obviously within even the intellectual resources of a haddock to answer, "But if a haddock is a horse, why should I yield to you any more than you to me? Why should that singing horse commonly called the nightingale, or that climbing horse hitherto known as the cat, fall down and worship you because of your horsehood? If all our native faculties are the accomplishments of a horse—why then you are only another horse without any accomplishments." When thus gently reasoned with, the horse flings up his heels, kicks the cat, crushes the oyster, eats the haddock and pursues the nightingale, and that is how the war began.

This apologue is not in the least more fantastic than the facts of the Teutonic claim. The Germans do really say that Englishmen are only Sea-Germans, as our haddocks were only sea-horses. They do really say that the nightingales of Tuscany or the pearls of Hellas must somehow be German birds or German jewels. They do maintain that the Italian Renaissance was really the German Renaissance, pure Germans having Italian names when they were painters, as cockneys sometimes have when they are hair-dressers. They suggest that Jesus and the great Jews were Teutonic. One Teutonist I read actually explained the fresh energy of the French Revolution and the stale privileges of its German enemies by saying that the Germanic soul awoke in France and attacked the Latin influence in Germany. On the advantages of this method I need not dwell: if you are annoyed at Jack Johnson knocking out an English prize-fighter, you have only to say that it was the whiteness of the black man that won and the blackness of the white man that was beaten. But about the Italian Renaissance they are less general and will go into detail. They will discover (in their researches into 'istry, as Mr. Gandish said) that Michael Angelo's surname was Buonarotti; and they will point out that the word "roth" is very like the word "rot." Which, in one sense, is true enough. Most Englishmen will be content to say it is all rot and pass on. It is all of a piece with the preposterous Prussian history, which talks, for instance, about the "perfect religious tolerance of the Goths"; which is like talking about the legal impartiality of chicken-pox. He will decline to believe that the Jews were Germans; though he may perhaps have met some Germans who were Jews. But deeper than any such practical reply, lies the deep inconsistency of the parable. It is simply this; that if Teutonism be used for comprehension it cannot be used for conquest. If all intelligent peoples are Germans, then Prussians are only the least intelligent Germans. If the men of Flanders are as German as the men of Frankfort, we can only say that in saving Belgium we are helping the Germans who are in the right against the Germans who are in the wrong. Thus in Alsace the conquerors are forced into the comic posture of annexing the people for being German and then persecuting them for being French. The French Teutons who built Rheims must surrender it to the South German Teutons who have partly built Cologne; and these in turn surrender Cologne to the North German Teutons, who never built anything, except the wooden Aunt Sally of old Hindenburg. Every Teuton must fall on his face before an inferior Teuton; until they all find, in the foul marshes towards the Baltic, the very lowest of all possible Teutons, and worship him—and find he is a Slav. So much for Pan-Germanism.

But though Teutonism is indefinable, or at least is by the Teutons undefined, it is not unreal. A vague but genuine soul does possess all peoples who boast of Teutonism; and has possessed ourselves, in so far as we have been touched by that folly. Not a race, but rather a religion, the thing exists; and in 1870 its sun was at noon. We can most briefly describe it under three heads.

The victory of the German arms meant before Leipzic, and means now, the overthrow of a certain idea. That idea is the idea of the Citizen. This is true in a quite abstract and courteous sense; and is not meant as a loose charge of oppression. Its truth is quite compatible with a view that the Germans are better governed than the French. In many ways the Germans are very well governed. But they might be governed ten thousand times better than they are, or than anybody ever can be, and still be as far as ever from governing. The idea of the Citizen is that his individual human nature shall be constantly and creatively active in *altering* the State. The Germans are right in regarding the idea as dangerously revolutionary. Every Citizen *is* a revolution.

That is, he destroys, devours and adapts his environment to the extent of his own thought and conscience. This is what separates the human social effort from the non-human; the bee creates the honey-comb, but he does not criticise it. The German ruler really does feed and train the German as carefully as a gardener waters a flower. But if the flower suddenly began to water the gardener, he would be much surprised. So in Germany the people really are educated; but in France the people educates. The French not only make up the State, but make the State; not only make it, but remake it. In Germany the ruler is the artist, always painting the happy German like a portrait; in France the Frenchman is the artist, always painting and repainting France like a house. No state of social good that does not mean the Citizen *choosing* good, as well as getting it, has the idea of the Citizen at all. To say the Germanies are naturally at war with this idea is merely to respect them and take them seriously: otherwise their war on the French Revolution would be only an ignorant feud. It is this, to them, risky and fanciful notion of the critical and creative Citizen, which in 1870 lay prostrate under United Germany— under the undivided hoof.

Nevertheless, when the German says he has or loves freedom, what he says is not false. He means something; and what he means is the second principle, which I may summarise as the Irresponsibility of Thought. Within the iron framework of the fixed State, the German has not only liberty but anarchy. Anything can be said although, or rather because, nothing can be done. Philosophy is really free. But this practically means only that the prisoner's cell has become the madman's cell: that it is scrawled all over inside with stars and systems, so that it looks like eternity. This is the contradiction remarked by Dr. Sarolea, in his brilliant book, between the wildness of German theory and the tameness of German practice. The Germans *sterilise* thought, making it active with a wild virginity; which can bear no fruit.

But though there are so many mad theories, most of them

have one root; and depend upon one assumption. It matters little whether we call it, with the German Socialists, "the Materialist Theory of History"; or, with Bismarck, "blood and iron." It can be put most fairly thus: that all *important* events of history are biological, like a change of pasture or the communism of a pack of wolves. Professors are still tearing their hair in the effort to prove somehow that the Crusaders were migrating for food like swallows; or that the French Revolutionists were somehow only swarming like bees. This works in two ways often accounted opposite; and explains both the German Socialist and the Junker. For, first, it fits in with Teutonic Imperialism; making the "blonde beasts" of Germania into lions whose nature it is to eat such lambs as the French. The highest success of this notion in Europe is marked by praise given to a race famous for its physical firmness and fighting breed, but which has frankly pillaged and scarcely pretended to rule; the Turk, whom some Tories called "the gentleman of Europe." The Kaiser paused to adore the Crescent on his way to patronise the Cross. It was corporately embodied when Greece attempted a solitary adventure against Turkey and was quickly crushed. That English guns helped to impose the mainly Germanic policy of the Concert upon Crete, cannot be left out of mind while we are making appeals to Greece—or considering the crimes of England.

But the same principle serves to keep the internal politics of the Germans quiet, and prevent Socialism being the practical hope or peril it has been in so many other countries. It operates in two ways; first, by a curious fallacy about "the time not being ripe"—as if *time* could ever be ripe. The same savage superstition from the forests had infected Matthew Arnold pretty badly when he made a personality out of the Zeitgeist—perhaps the only ghost that was ever entirely fabulous. It is tricked by a biological parallel, by which the chicken always comes out of the egg "at the right time." He does not; he comes out when he comes out. The Marxian Socialist will not strike till the clock strikes; and the clock is made in Germany, and never strikes. Moreover, the theory of all history as a search for food makes the masses content with having food and physic, but not freedom. The best working model in the matter is the system of Compulsory Insurance; which was a total failure and dead letter in France but has been, in the German sense, a great success in Germany. It treats employed persons as a fixed, separate, and lower caste, who must not themselves dispose of the margin of their small wages. In 1911 it was introduced into England by Mr. Lloyd George, who had studied its operations in Germany, and, by the Prussian prestige in "social reform," was passed.

These three tendencies cohere, or are cohering, in an institution which is not without a great historical basis and not without great modern conveniences. And as France was the standard-bearer of citizenship in 1798, Germany is the standard-bearer of this alternative solution in 1915. The institution which our fathers called Slavery fits in with, or rather logically flows from, all the three spirits of which I have spoken, and promises great advantages to each of them. It can give the individual worker everything except the power to alter the State—that is, his own status. Finality (or what certain eleutheromaniacs would call hopelessness) of status is the soul of Slavery—and of Compulsory Insurance. Then again, Germany gives the individual exactly the liberty that has always been given to a slave—the liberty to think, the liberty to dream, the liberty to rage; the liberty to indulge in any intellectual hypotheses about the unalterable world and state—such as have always been free to slaves, from the stoical maxims of Epictetus to the skylarking fairy tales of Uncle Remus. And it has been truly urged by all defenders of slavery that, if history has merely a material test, the material condition of the subordinate under slavery tends to be good rather than bad. When I once pointed out how precisely the "model village" of a great employer reproduces the safety and seclusion of an old slave estate, the employer thought it quite enough to answer indignantly that he had provided baths, playing-grounds, a theatre, etc., for his workers. He would probably have thought it odd to hear a planter in South Carolina boast that he had provided banjos, hymn-books, and places suitable for the cake-walk. Yet the planter must have provided the banjos, for a slave cannot own property. And if this Germanic sociology is indeed to prevail among us, I think some of the broad-minded thinkers who concur in its prevalence owe something like an apology to many gallant gentlemen whose graves lie where the last battle was fought in the Wilderness; men who had the courage to fight for it, the courage to die for it and, above all, the courage to call it by its name.

With the acceptance by England of the German Insurance Act, I bring this sketch of the past relations of the two countries to an end. I have written this book because I wish, once and for all, to be done with my friend Professor Whirlwind of Prussia, who has long despaired of really defending his own country, and has fallen back upon abusing mine. He has dropped, amid general derision, his attempt to call a thing right when even the Chancellor who did it called it wrong. But he has an idea that if he can show that somebody from England somewhere did another wrong, the two wrongs may make a right. Against the cry of the Roman Catholic Poles the Prussian has never done, or even pretended to do, anything but harden his heart; but he has (such are the lovable inconsistencies of human nature) a warm corner in his heart for the Roman Catholic Irish. He has not a word to say for himself about the campaign in Belgium, but he still has many wise, reproachful words to utter about the campaign in South Africa. I propose to take those words out of his mouth. I will have nothing to do with the fatuous front-bench pretensions that our governors always govern well, that our statesmen are never whitewashed and never in need of whitewash. The only moral superiority I claim is that of not defending the indefensible. I most earnestly urge my countrymen not to hide behind thin official excuses, which the sister kingdoms and the subject races can easily see through. We can confess that our crimes have been as mountains, and still not be afraid of the present comparison. There may be, in the eyes of some, a risk in dwelling in this dark hour on our failures in the past: I believe profoundly that the risk is all the other way. I believe that the most deadly danger to our arms to-day lies in any whiff of that self-praise, any flavour of that moral cowardice, any glimpse of that impudent and ultimate impenitence, that may make one Boer or Scot or Welshman or Irishman or Indian feel that he is only smoothing the path for a second Prussia. I have passed the great part of my life in criticising and condemning the existing rulers and institutions of my country: I think it is infinitely the most patriotic thing that a man can do. I have no illusions either about our past or our present. *I* think our whole history in Ireland has been a vulgar and ignorant hatred of the crucifix, expressed by a crucifixion. I think the South African War was a dirty work which we did under the whips of moneylenders. I think Mitchelstown was a disgrace; I think Denshawi was a devilry.

Yet there is one part of life and history in which I would assert the absolute spotlessness of England. In one department we wear a robe of white and a halo of innocence. Long and weary as may be the records of our wickedness, in one direction we have done nothing but good. Whoever we may have wronged, we have never wronged Germany. Again and again we have dragged her from under the just vengeance of her enemies, from the holy anger of Maria Teresa, from the impatient and contemptuous common sense of Napoleon. We have kept a ring fence around the Germans while they sacked Denmark and dismembered France. And if we had served our God as we have served *their* kings, there would not be to-day one remnant of them in our path, either to slander or to slay us.

CHAPTER IX

THE AWAKENING OF ENGLAND

In October 1912 silent and seemingly uninhabited crags and chasms in the high western region of the Balkans echoed and re-echoed with a single shot. It was fired by the hand of a king—real king, who sat listening to his people in front of his own house (for it was hardly a palace), and who, in consequence of his listening to the people, not unfrequently imprisoned the politicians. It is said of him that his great respect for Gladstone as the western advocate of Balkan freedom was slightly shadowed by the fact that Gladstone did not succeed in effecting the bodily capture of Jack the Ripper. This simple monarch knew that if a malefactor were the terror of the mountain hamlets, his subjects would expect him personally to take arms and pursue the ruffian; and if he refused to do so, would very probably experiment with another king. And the same primitive conception of a king being kept for some kind of purpose, led them also to expect him to lead in a foreign campaign, and it was with his own hand that he fired the first shot of the war which brought down into the dust the ancient empire of the Grand Turk.

His kingdom was little more than the black mountain after which it was named: we commonly refer to it under its Italian translation of Montenegro. It is worth while to pause for a moment upon his picturesque and peculiar community, because it is perhaps the simplest working model of all that stood in the path of the great Germanic social machine I have described in the last chapter—stood in its path and was soon to be very nearly destroyed by its onset. It was a branch of the Serbian stock which had climbed into this almost inaccessible eyrie, and thence, for many hundred years, had mocked at the predatory empire of the Turks. The Serbians in their turn were but one branch of the peasant Slavs, millions of whom are spread over Russia and subject on many sides to empires with which they have less sympathy; and the Slavs again, in the broad features which are important here, are not merely Slavonic but simply European. But a particular picture is generally more pointed and intelligible than tendencies which elsewhere are mingled with subtler tendencies; and of this unmixed European simplicity Montenegro is an excellent model.

Moreover, the instance of one small Christian State will serve to emphasise that this is not a quarrel between England and Germany, but between Europe and Germany. It is my whole purpose in these pages not to spare my own country where it is open to criticism; and I freely admit that Montenegro, morally and politically speaking, is almost as much in advance of England as it is of Germany. In Montenegro there are no millionaires—and therefore next to no Socialists. As to why there are no millionaires, it is a mystery, and best studied among the mysteries of the Middle Ages. By some of the dark ingenuities of that age of priestcraft a curious thing was discovered—that if you kill every usurer, every forestaller, every adulterater, every user of false weights, every fixer of false boundaries, every land-thief, every water-thief, you afterwards discover by a strange indirect miracle, or disconnected truth from heaven, that you have no millionaires. Without dwelling further on this dark matter, we may say that this great gap in the Montenegrin experience explains the other great gap—the lack of Socialists. The Class-conscious Proletarian of All Lands is curiously absent from this land. The reason (I have sometimes fancied) is that the Proletarian is class-conscious, not because he is a Proletarian of All Lands, but because he is a Proletarian with no lands. The poor people in Montenegro have lands—not landlords. They have roots; for the peasant is the root of the priest, the poet, and the warrior. And *this*, and not a mere recrimination about acts of violence, is the ground of the age-long Balkan bitterness against the Turkish conqueror. Montenegrins are patriotic for Montenegro; but Turks are not patriotic for Turkey. They never heard of it, in fact. They are Bedouins, as homeless as the desert. The "wrong horse" of Lord Salisbury was an Arab steed, only stabled in Byzantium. It is hard enough to rule vagabond people, like the gypsies. To be ruled by them is impossible.

Nevertheless what was called the nineteenth century, and named with a sort of transcendental faith (as in a Pythagorean worship of number), was wearing to its close with reaction everywhere, and the Turk, the great type of reaction, stronger than ever in the saddle. The most civilised of the Christian nations overshadowed by the Crescent dared to attack it and was overwhelmed in a catastrophe that seemed as unanswerable as Hittin. In England Gladstone and Gladstonism were dead; and Mr. Kipling, a less mystical Carlyle, was expending a type of praise upon the British Army which would have been even more appropriate to the Prussian Army. The Prussian Army ruled Prussia; Prussia ruled Germany; Germany ruled the Concert of Europe. She was planting everywhere the appliances of that new servile machinery which was her secret; the absolute identification of national subordination with business employment; so that Krupp could count on Kaiser and Kaiser on Krupp. Every other commercial traveller was pathetically proud of being both a slave and a spy. The old and the new tyrants had taken hands. The "sack" of the boss was as silent and fatal as the sack of the Bosphorus. And the dream of the citizen was at an end.

It was under a sky so leaden and on a road so strewn with bones that the little mountain democracy with its patriarchal prince went out, first and before all its friends, on the last and seemingly the most hopeless of the rebellions against the Ottoman Empire. Only one of the omens seemed other than disastrous; and even that was doubtful. For the successful

Mediterranean attack on Tripoli while proving the gallantry of the Italians (if that ever needed proving) could be taken in two ways, and was seen by many, and probably most, sincere liberals as a mere extension of the Imperialist reaction of Bosnia and Paardeberg, and not as the promise of newer things. Italy, it must be remembered, was still supposed to be the partner of Prussia and the Hapsburgs. For days that seemed like months the microscopic state seemed to be attempting alone what the Crusades had failed to accomplish. And for days Europe and the great powers were thunderstruck, again and yet again, by the news of Turkish forts falling, Turkish cohorts collapsing, the unconquerable Crescent going down in blood. The Serbians, the Bulgarians, the Greeks had gathered and risen from their lairs; and men knew that these peasants had done what all the politicians had long despaired of doing, and that the spirit of the first Christian Emperor was already standing over the city that is named after his name.

For Germany this quite unexpected rush was a reversal of the whole tide of the world. It was as if the Rhine itself had returned from the ocean and retired into the Alps. For a long time past every important political process in Europe had been produced or permitted by Prussia. She had pulled down ministers in France and arrested reforms in Russia. Her ruler was acclaimed by Englishmen like Rhodes, and Americans like Roosevelt, as the great prince of the age. One of the most famous and brilliant of our journalists called him "the Lord Chief Justice of Europe." He was the strongest man in Christendom; and he had confirmed and consecrated the Crescent. And when he had consecrated it a few hill tribes had risen and trampled it like mire. One or two other things about the same time, less important in themselves, struck in the Prussian's ear the same new note of warning and doubt. He sought to obtain a small advantage on the north-west coast of Africa; and England seemed to show a certain strange stiffness in insisting on its abandonment. In the councils over Morocco, England agreed with France with what did not seem altogether an accidental agreement. But we shall not be wrong if we put the crucial point of the German surprise and anger at the attack from the Balkans and the fall of Adrianople. Not only did it menace the key of Asia and the whole Eastern dream of German commerce; not only did it offer the picture of one army trained by France and victorious, and another army trained by Germany and beaten. There was more than the material victory of the Creusot over the Krupp gun. It was also the victory of the peasant's field over the Krupp factory. By this time there was in the North German brain an awful inversion of all the legends and heroic lives that the human race has loved. Prussia *hated* romance. Chivalry was not a thing she neglected; it was a thing that tormented her as any bully is tormented by an unanswered challenge. That weird process was completed of which I have spoken on an earlier page, whereby the soul of this strange people was everywhere on the side of the dragon against the knight, of the giant against the hero. Anything unexpected—the forlorn hopes, the eleventh-hour inspirations, by which the weak can elude the strong, and which take the hearts of happier men like trumpets—filled the Prussian with a cold fury, as of a frustrated fate. The Prussian felt as a Chicago pork butcher would feel if the pigs not only refused to pass through his machine, but turned into romantic wild boars, raging and rending, calling for the old hunting of princes and fit to be the crests of kings.

The Prussian saw these things and his mind was made up. He was silent; but he laboured: laboured for three long years without intermission at the making of a military machine that should cut out of the world for ever such romantic accident or random adventure; a machine that should cure the human pigs for ever of any illusion that they had wings. That he did so plot and prepare for an attack that should come from him, anticipating and overwhelming any resistance, is now, even in the documents he has himself published, a fact of common sense. Suppose a man sells all his lands except a small yard containing a well; suppose in the division of the effects of an old friend he particularly asks for his razors; suppose when a corded trunk is sent him he sends back the trunk, but keeps the cord. And then suppose we hear that a rival of his has been lassoed with a rope, his throat then cut, apparently with a razor, and his body hidden in a well, we do not call in Sherlock Holmes to project a preliminary suspicion about the guilty party. In the discussions held by the Prussian Government with Lord Haldane and Sir Edward Grey we can now see quite as plainly the meaning of the things that were granted and the things that were withheld, the things that would have satisfied the Prussian plotter and the things that did not satisfy him. The German Chancellor refused an English promise not to be aggressive and asked instead for an English promise to be neutral. There is no meaning in the distinction, except in the mind of an aggressor. Germany proposed a pacific arrangement which forbade England to form a fighting alliance with France, but permitted Germany to retain her old fighting alliance with Austria. When the hour of war came she used Austria, used the old fighting alliance and tried to use the new idea of English neutrality. That is to say, she used the rope, the razor, and the well.

But it was either by accident or by individual diplomatic skill that England at the end of the three years even had her own hands free to help in frustrating the German plot. The mass of the English people had no notion of such a plot; and indeed regarded the occasional suggestion of it as absurd. Nor did even the people who knew best know very much better. Thanks and even apologies are doubtless due to those who in the deepest lull of our sleeping partnership with Prussia saw her not as a partner but a potential enemy; such men as Mr. Blatchford, Mr. Bart Kennedy, or the late Emil Reich. But there is a distinction to be made. Few even of these, with the admirable and indeed almost magical exception of Dr. Sarolea, saw Germany as she was; occupied mainly with Europe and only incidentally with England; indeed, in the first stages, not occupied with England at all. Even the Anti-Germans were too insular. Even those who saw most of Germany's plan saw too much of England's part in it. They saw it almost wholly as a commercial and colonial quarrel; and saw its issue under the image of an invasion of England, which is even now not very probable. This fear of Germany was indeed a very German fear of Germany. This also conceived the English as Sea-Germans. It conceived Germany as at war with something like itself—practical, prosaic, capitalist, competitive Germany, prepared to cut us up in battle as she cut us out in business. The time of our larger vision was not yet, when we should realise that Germany was more deeply at war with things quite unlike herself, things from which we also had sadly strayed. Then we should remember what we were and see whence we also had come; and far and high upon that mountain from which the Crescent was cast down, behold what was everywhere the real enemy of the Iron Cross—the peasant's cross, which is of wood.

Even our very slight ripples of panic, therefore, were provincial, and even shallow; and for the most part we were possessed and convinced of peace. That peace was not a noble one. We had indeed reached one of the lowest and flattest levels of all our undulating history; and it must be admitted that the contemptuous calculation with which Germany counted on our submission and abstention was not altogether unfounded, though it was, thank God, unfulfilled. The full fruition of our alliances against freedom had come. The meek acceptance of Kultur in our books and schools had stiffened what was once a free country with a German formalism and a German fear. By a queer irony, even the same popular writer who had already warned us against the Prussians, had sought to preach among the populace a very Prussian fatalism, pivoted upon the importance of the charlatan Haeckel. The wrestle of the two great parties had long slackened into an embrace. The fact was faintly denied, and a pretence was still made that no pact: existed beyond a common patriotism. But the pretence failed altogether; for it was evident that the leaders on either side, so far from leading in divergent directions, were much closer to each other than to their own followers. The power of these leaders had enormously increased; but the distance between them had diminished, or, rather, disappeared. It was said about 1800, in derision of the Foxite rump, that the Whig Party came down to Parliament in a four-wheeler. It might literally be said in 1900 that the Whig Party and the Tory Party came to Parliament in a hansom cab. It was not a case of two towers rising into different roofs or spires, but founded in the same soil. It was rather the case of an arch, of which the foundation-stones on either side might fancy they were two buildings; but the stones nearest the keystone would know there was only one. This "two-handed engine" still stood ready to strike, not, indeed, the other part of itself, but anyone who ventured to deny that it was doing so. We were ruled, as it were, by a Wonderland king and queen, who cut off our heads, not for saying they quarrelled but for saying they didn't. The libel law was now used, not to crush lies about private life, but to crush truths about public life. Representation had become mere misrepresentation; a maze of loopholes. This was mainly due to the monstrous presence of certain secret moneys, on which alone many men could win the ruinous elections of the age, and which were contributed and distributed with less check or record than is tolerated in the lowest trade or club. Only one or two people attacked these funds; nobody defended them. Through them the great capitalists had the handle of politics, as of everything else. The poor were struggling hopelessly against rising prices; and their attempts at collective bargaining, by the collective refusal of badly-paid work, were discussed in the press, Liberal and Tory, as attacks upon the State. And so they were; upon the Servile State.

Such was the condition of England in 1914, when Prussia, now at last armed to the teeth and secure of triumph, stood up before the world, and solemnly, like one taking a sacrament, consecrated her campaign with a crime. She entered by a forbidden door, one which she had herself forbidden—marching upon France through neutralised Belgium, where every step was on her broken word. Her neutralised neighbours resisted, as indeed they, like ourselves, were pledged to do. Instantly the whole invasion was lit up with a flame of moral lunacy, that turned the watching nations white who had never known the Prussian. The statistics of non-combatants killed and tortured by this time only stun the imagination. But two friends of my own have been in villages sacked by the Prussian march. One saw a tabernacle containing the Sacrament patiently picked out in pattern by shot after shot. The other saw a rocking-horse and the wooden toys in a nursery laboriously hacked to pieces. Those two facts together will be enough to satisfy some of us of the name of the Spirit that had passed.

And then a strange thing happened. England, that had not in the modern sense any army at all, was justified of all her children. Respected institutions and reputations did indeed waver and collapse on many sides: though the chief of the states replied worthily to a bribe from the foreign bully, many other politicians were sufficiently wild and weak, though doubtless patriotic in intention. One was set to restrain the journalists, and had to be restrained himself, for being more sensational than any of them. Another scolded the working-classes in the style of an intoxicated temperance lecturer. But England was saved by a forgotten thing—the English. Simple men with simple motives, the chief one a hate of injustice which grows simpler the longer we stare at it, came out of their dreary tenements and their tidy shops, their fields and their suburbs and their factories and their rookeries, and asked for the arms of men. In a throng that was at last three million men, the islanders went forth from their island, as simply as the mountaineers had gone forth from their mountain, with their faces to the dawn.

CHAPTER X

THE BATTLE OF THE MARNE

The impression produced by the first week of war was that the British contingent had come just in time for the end of the world. Or rather, for any sensitive and civilised man, touched by the modern doubt but by the equally modern mysticism, that old theocratic vision fell far short of the sickening terror of the time. For it was a day of judgment in which upon the throne in heaven and above the cherubim, sat not God, but another.

The British had been posted at the extreme western end of the allied line in the north. The other end rested on the secure city and fortress of Namur; their end rested upon nothing. It is not wholly a sentimental fancy to say that there was something forlorn in the position of that loose end in a strange land, with only the sad fields of Northern France between them and the sea. For it was really round that loose end that the foe would probably fling the lasso of his charge; it was here that death might soon be present upon every side. It must be remembered that many critics, including many Englishmen, doubted whether a rust had not eaten into this as into other parts of the national life, feared that England had too long neglected both the ethic and the technique of war, and would prove a weak link in the chain. The enemy was absolutely certain that it was so. To these men, standing disconsolately amid the hedgeless plains and poplars, came the news that Namur was gone, which was to their captains one of the four corners of the earth. The two armies had touched; and instantly the weaker took an electric shock which told of electric energy, deep into deep Germany, battery behind battery of abysmal force. In the instant it was discovered that the enemy was more numerous than they had dreamed. He was actually more numerous even than they discovered. Every oncoming horseman doubled as in a drunkard's vision; and they were soon striving without speech in a nightmare of numbers. Then all the allied forces at the front were overthrown in the tragic battle of Mons; and began that black retreat, in which so many of our young men knew war first and at its worst in this terrible world; and so many never returned.

In that blackness began to grow strange emotions, long unfamiliar to our blood. Those six dark days are as full of legends as the six centuries of the Dark Ages. Many of these may be exaggerated fancies, one was certainly an avowed fiction, others are quite different from it and more difficult to dissipate into the daylight. But one curious fact remains about them if they were all lies, or even if they were all deliberate works of art. Not one of them referred to those close, crowded, and stirring three centuries which are nearest to us, and which alone are covered in this sketch, the centuries during which the Teutonic influence had expanded itself over our islands. Ghosts were there perhaps, but they were the ghosts of forgotten ancestors. Nobody saw Cromwell or even Wellington; nobody so much as thought about Cecil Rhodes. Things were either seen or said among the British which linked them up, in matters deeper than any alliance, with the French, who spoke of Joan of Arc in heaven above the fated city; or the Russians who dreamed of the Mother of God with her hand pointing to the west. They were the visions or the inventions of a mediæval army; and a prose poet was in line with many popular rumours when he told of ghostly archers crying "Array, Array," as in that long-disbanded yeomanry in which I have fancied Cobbett as carrying a bow. Other tales, true or only symptomatic, told of one on a great white horse who was not the victor of Blenheim or even the Black Prince, but a faint figure out of far-off martyrologies—St. George. One soldier is asserted to have claimed to identify the saint because he was "on every quid." On the coins, St. George is a Roman soldier.

But these fancies, if they were fancies, might well seem the last sickly flickerings of an old-world order now finally wounded to the death. That which was coming on, with the whole weight of a new world, was something that had never been numbered among the Seven Champions of Christendom. Now, in more doubtful and more hopeful days, it is almost impossible to repicture what was, for those who understood, the gigantic finality of the first German strides. It seemed as if the forces of the ancient valour fell away to right and left; and there opened a grand, smooth granite road right to the gate of Paris, down which the great Germania moved like a tall, unanswerable sphinx, whose pride could destroy all things and survive them. In her train moved, like moving mountains, Cyclopean guns that had never been seen among men, before which walled cities melted like wax, their mouths set insolently upwards as if threatening to besiege the sun. Nor is it fantastic to speak so of the new and abnormal armaments; for the soul of Germany was really expressed in colossal wheels and cylinders; and her guns were more symbolic than her flags. Then and now, and in every place and time, it is to be noted that the German superiority has been in a certain thing and of a certain kind. It is *not* unity; it is not, in the moral sense, discipline. Nothing can be more united in a moral sense than a French, British, or Russian regiment. Nothing, for that matter, could be more united than a Highland clan at Killiecrankie or a rush of religious fanatics in the Soudan. What such engines, in such size and multiplicity, really meant was this: they meant a type of life naturally intolerable to happier and more healthy-minded men, conducted on a larger scale and consuming larger populations than had ever been known before. They meant cities growing larger than provinces, factories growing larger than cities; they meant the empire of the slum. They meant a degree of detailed repetition and dehumanised division of labour, to which no man born would surrender his brief span in the sunshine, if he could hope to beat his ploughshare into a sword. The nations of the earth were not to surrender to the Kaiser; they were to surrender to Krupp, his master and theirs; the French, the British, the Russians were to surrender to Krupp as the Germans themselves, after a few swiftly broken strikes, had already surrendered to Krupp. Through every cogwheel in that incomparable machinery, through every link in that iron and unending chain, ran the mastery and the skill of a certain kind of artist; an artist whose hands are never idle through dreaming or drawn back in disgust or lifted in wonder or in wrath; but sure and tireless in their touch upon the thousand little things that make the invisible machinery of life. That artist was there in triumph; but he had no name. The ancient world called him the Slave.

From this advancing machine of millions, the slighter array of the Allies, and especially the British at their ultimate outpost, saved themselves by a succession of hair's-breadth escapes and what must have seemed to the soldiers the heartrending luck of a mouse before a cat. Again and again Von Kluck's cavalry, supported by artillery and infantry, clawed round the end of the British force, which eluded it as by leaping back again and again. Sometimes the pursuer was, so to speak, so much on top of his prey that it could not even give way to him; but had to hit such blows as it could in the hope of checking him for the instant needed for escape. Sometimes the oncoming wave was so close that a small individual accident, the capture of one man, would mean the washing out of a whole battalion. For day after day this living death endured. And day after day a certain dark truth began to be revealed, bit by bit, certainly to the incredulous wonder of the Prussians, quite possibly to the surprise of the French, and quite as possibly to the surprise of themselves; that there was something singular about the British soldiers. That singular thing may be expressed in a variety of ways; but it would be almost certainly expressed insufficiently by anyone who had not had the moral courage to face the facts about his country in the last decades before the war. It may perhaps be best expressed by saying that some thousands of Englishmen were dead: and that England was not.

The fortress of Maubeuge had gaped, so to speak, offering a refuge for the unresting and tormented retreat; the British Generals had refused it and continued to fight a losing fight in the open for the sake of the common plan. At night an enormous multitude of Germans had come unexpectedly through the forest and caught a smaller body of the British in Landrecies; failed to dislodge them and lost a whole battalion in that battle of the darkness. At the extreme end of the line Smith-Dorrien's division, who seemed to be nearly caught or cut off, had fought with one gun against four, and so hammered the Germans that they were forced to let go their hold; and the British were again free. When the blowing up of a bridge announced that they had crossed the last river, something other than that battered remnant was saved; it was the honour of the thing by which we live.

The driven and defeated line stood at last almost under the walls of Paris; and the world waited for the doom of the city. The gates seemed to stand open; and the Prussian was to ride into it for the third and the last time: for the end of its long epic of liberty and equality was come. And still the very able and very French individual on whom rested the last hope of the seemingly hopeless Alliance stood unruffled as a rock, in every angle of his sky-blue jacket and his bulldog figure. He had called his bewildered soldiers back when they had broken the invasion at Guise; he had silently digested the responsibility of dragging on the retreat, as in despair, to the last desperate leagues before the capital; and he stood and watched. And even as he watched the whole huge invasion swerved.

Out through Paris and out and around beyond Paris, other men in dim blue coats swung out in long lines upon the plain, slowly folding upon Von Kluck like blue wings. Von Kluck stood an instant; and then, flinging a few secondary forces to delay the wing that was swinging round on him, dashed across the Allies' line at a desperate angle, to smash it in the centre as with a hammer. It was less desperate than it seemed; for he counted, and might well count, on the moral and physical bankruptcy of the British line and the end of the French line immediately in front of him, which for six days and nights he had chased before him like autumn leaves before a whirlwind. Not unlike autumn leaves, red-stained, dust-hued, and tattered, they lay there as if swept into a corner. But even as their conquerors wheeled eastwards, their bugles blew the charge; and the English went forward through the wood that is called Creçy, and stamped it with their seal for the second time, in the highest moment of all the secular history of man.

But it was not now the Creçy in which English and French knights had met in a more coloured age, in a battle that was rather a tournament. It was a league of all knights for the remains of all knighthood, of all brotherhood in arms or in arts, against that which is and has been radically unknightly and radically unbrotherly from the beginning. Much was to happen after—murder and flaming folly and madness in earth and sea and sky; but all men knew in their hearts that the third Prussian thrust had failed, and Christendom was delivered once more. The empire of blood and iron rolled slowly back towards the darkness of the northern forests; and the great nations of the West went forward; where side by side as after a long lover's quarrel, went the ensigns of St. Denys and St. George.

NOTE ON THE WORD "ENGLISH"

The words "England" and "English" as used here require a word of explanation, if only to anticipate the ire of the inevitable Scot. To begin with, the word "British" involves a similar awkwardness. I have tried to use it in the one or two cases that referred to such things as military glory and unity: though I am sure I have failed of full consistency in so complex a matter. The difficulty is that this sense of glory and unity, which should certainly cover the Scotch, should also cover the Irish. And while it is fairly safe to call a Scotsman a North Briton (despite the just protest of Stevenson), it is very unsafe indeed to call an Irishman a West Briton. But there is a deeper difficulty. I can assure the Scot that I say "England," not because I deny Scottish nationality, but because I affirm it. And I can say, further, that I could not here include Scots in the thesis, simply because I could not include them in the condemnation. This book is a study, not of a disease but rather of a weakness, which has only been predominant in the predominant partner. It would not be true, for instance, to say either of Ireland or Scotland that the populace lacked a religion; but I do think that British policy as a whole has suffered from the English lack of one, with its inevitable result of plutocracy and class contempt.

Made in the USA
Middletown, DE
04 January 2024

47191087R00057